William Copeland Borlase

Nænia Cornubiæ

A descriptive essay, illustrative of the sepulchres and funereal customs of the early inhabitants of the county of Cornwall

William Copeland Borlase

Nænia Cornubiæ
A descriptive essay, illustrative of the sepulchres and funereal customs of the early inhabitants of the county of Cornwall

ISBN/EAN: 9783337018689

Printed in Europe, USA, Canada, Australia, Japan

Cover: Foto ©ninafisch / pixelio.de

More available books at **www.hansebooks.com**

Nænia Cornubiæ,

A DESCRIPTIVE ESSAY,

ILLUSTRATIVE OF THE SEPULCHRES AND FUNEREAL CUSTOMS OF THE EARLY INHABITANTS OF THE COUNTY OF CORNWALL.

"Sunt * * quorum non est recordatio, qui perierunt quasi non extitissent, et fuerunt quasi non fuissent, liberique ipsorum post ipsos."
Ecclus, cap. LI.

BY

WILLIAM COPELAND BORLASE, B.A., F.S.A.

LONDON:
LONGMANS, GREEN, READER, AND DYER.
TRURO: J. R. NETHERTON.

1872.

TO

JOHN JOPE ROGERS, Esq.,

OF PENROSE, IN THE COUNTY OF CORNWALL,

PRESIDENT OF THE ROYAL INSTITUTION OF CORNWALL

DURING THE YEARS 1868 AND 1869,

THE AUTHOR DEDICATES THIS LITTLE WORK;

AN INADEQUATE, THOUGH A GRATEFUL, ACKNOWLEDGEMENT OF THE

KIND INTEREST HE HAS ALWAYS TAKEN

IN THE PURSUITS OF A YOUNG ANTIQUARY.

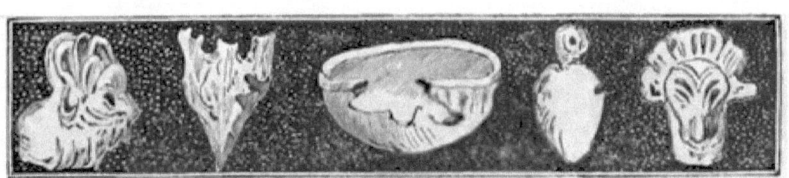

Introductory Preface.

❖❖❖❖❖❖❖❖

IT is not without great deference that the Author presents his readers with the following notices of the Primitive Sepulchral Monuments of his native county. Living in the midst of these remains, and possessing, through the kind courtesy of the landed proprietors, every facility for extending his researches to those tumuli previously unexplored, he has amused himself by collecting together the materials from which these pages are now compiled. But when comparing the small amount of inductive evidence he has thus far been able to obtain, with the exhaustive compendium of facts brought by Mr. Bateman from the barrows of Derbyshire and Yorkshire, or with the extensive researches of Sir R. C. Hoare, and others who have devoted themselves to the task of solving the mystery of the burial mounds, each in his own district, he cannot but feel that his work, when he has done all, must be, at best, but brief and deficient. If, however, it will aid in the work of classifying the entire series of sepulchral remains, scattered throughout the British Isles, the first object will at least be gained; and, much more will this be the case, should the perusal of it lead others to follow in the track, and preserve from oblivion those relics of a "speechless past," which are daily falling a prey to the pickaxe or the plough.

In the minute and somewhat lengthy details which accompany some of the descriptions, the ordinary reader will find a considerable trial of his patience. But the Critic and the Antiquary will know how to pardon this fault, when they reflect that it is only by the accumulation and juxtaposition of such apparently worthless minutiæ, that any one single *fact* can possibly be obtained, illustrative of the rude funereal customs practised in what may fairly be called the darkest age.

Many causes have been at work in Cornwall to make the task of gaining any detailed accounts of barrows previously searched one of peculiar difficulty; and the student must rely chiefly on such observations as he can himself personally make in the case of the few that still seem untouched. Until the last few years, very few persons, even of the better class, dreamed of preserving their discoveries at all: much less did they deem them worthy of a written account. Thus it has happened that out of the many thousand barrows strewn over the wilder portions of the Duchy, more than one half have been opened, as a mere matter of curiosity, by persons leaving no record whatever of the result. In other cases, where urns have actually been preserved and deposited in one of the two local Museums, the descriptions accompanying them are totally insufficient, and in a few instances are even mislaid and lost. Added to all this, the recent reclamation of waste-lands, particularly in the Western district, and the ever-fluctuating mineral interests, which literally turn the surface of the country inside out for miles together, have combined to obliterate those traces of the ancient inhabitants, which, when duly recorded and fitted together like a Chinese puzzle, make up the sum total of all that can ever be known about them. Yet, heavy as the "hand of ruin" has been laid on them, many a relic still remains to attest the fact that in the days of old, men were dwelling where we dwell, driving their flocks to pasture in the morning and in the evening to their pens, warring with the enemy or weeping over the slain. And thus, on those same wild granite hills, where in the winter time the sportsman may delight himself in the destruction of the living, the antiquary during many a long summer's day may engage himself, perhaps almost as pleasurably, in the resuscitation of the dead; clothing, where he can, in the mantle of history, those memorials of the past, which accident or previous acquaintance with them may have thrown in his path.

In the course of the following essay, it must be understood that no monuments are mentioned, unless incidentally, but those in which either interments have actually occurred, or where a sepulchral origin is placed beyond doubt by their form, or by a comparison with similar remains in the same or a kindred district. The objects engraved are also, almost invariably, those discovered in close proximity to the interments. Barrows and Cairns, however, are by no means the most fruitful field for Cornish Antiquities.[1] Tin stream-works, and the sites of ancient mines and smelting-houses, have been always the most productive source of objects of interest to the Cornish Antiquary; and a paper of considerable length and no little interest might be written on the subject of the implements, weapons, and ornaments of the ancient miners of the West.[2] With these, however, the present treatise has nothing to do; and it will be sufficient at present for the reader to discover that the promise held out by the title of this little volume has been very incompletely fulfilled. Of this the author is well aware. Much remains to be done; nooks and corners in the county there are, which still require investigation; but, should these pages meet with the reader's approbation, the author of them can only add that he intends to continue his researches, and to embody in a second series,

---

[1] Two gold *lunulæ* were, indeed, found in a mound of earth near Padstow, but not in connection with any sepulchral remains. The only instance where that precious metal has occurred actually *with* human bones will be duly described in the sequel.

[2] Carew mentions that in the stream-works are found "little tools heads of brass, which some term thunder axes." Besides these celts, bronze spearheads, arrow-heads, ornaments of gold, and jet, &c., &c. are among the objects not unfrequently dug up in the "old men's workings."

not only the unpublished accounts of several other barrows already explored by him, but also the details of any more, which he may be so fortunate as to obtain permission to investigate.

And here he must record his best thanks to those who have already granted him leave to make researches on their lands. In every instance, to apply for has only been to obtain, in the kindest of terms, an unqualified permission.

The deep obligations he is under to those who have preceded him in the work of publishing the accounts of investigations in the Cornish tumuli will be duly acknowledged in their proper place. From their works and papers much valuable matter has necessarily been borrowed, in order to make the essay at all complete.

To John Evans, Esq., F.R.S., to Sir Edward Smirke, and to the Society of Antiquaries, the author is indebted for permission to reproduce drawings from their works; while to the Rev. Canon Greenwell, of Durham, F.S.A., and to Albert Way, Esq., F.S.A., he must express his especial thanks for their goodness in replying to several troublesome Antiquarian queries.

To the labours of Mr. J. T. Blight, F.S.A., he owes a considerable debt of gratitude; nor must he forget to bear testimony to the excellent manner in which his brother, Mr. Joseph Blight, has carried out the important share of the work (viz., the wood engravings,) allotted to him.

Some apology is due to the reader for the "errata." These have been caused by the fact, that the author was travelling about at the time when the proof was passing through his hands, and therefore could not always give it the undivided attention he should have wished.

CONTENTS AND PLAN OF THE ESSAY.

❖ ❖ ❖ ❖ ❖ ❖ ❖ ❖ ❖

	PAGE.
The Study of Archæology—its aim and tendencies—remarks on the applicability of the theory of the 'Ages' to Cornish sepulchral interments—the Druids	1
Primitive Sepulchres—THE DOLMEN OR CROMLECH—The Cromlech divided into three classes, viz: *(a)* The Cromlech proper—*(b)* The larger Kist-Vaen—*(c)* The open Kist-Vaen, or Cenotaph	13
(a) The Cromlech proper—Instance of at Lanyon—Earth-cut grave found under	16
Interments divided into three classes, viz: (1) *Extended Inhumation*, (2) *Contracted Inhumation*, and (3) *Cremation*	19
I. EXTENDED INHUMATION, instances of, extremely rare ...	20
Earth-cut graves—Trewren, Trigganeris	22
Caerwynen, the second example of a Cromlech proper	24
(b) The larger Kist-Vaen—origin of—contained inhumated interments; and, where long and narrow, in all probability extended interments	27

	PAGE
Pawton Cromlech	32
Stone graves—at Samson—at the Land's End—at Botrea—at Bosavern—at the Cheesewring—and at Godolphin	34
Larger Kist-Vaens in which the mode of primary interment is doubtful — Lower Lanyon — Trethevy — Zennor—Chywoone—Mulfra—Quoit, St. Columb—Bosporthennis	42
Chambered Tumuli—compared with the Swedish examples—Giants' graves at Scilly—at Treryn—at Chapel Euny	69

II. CONTRACTED INHUMATION, instances of, also excessively rare—doubtful examples—Morvah Hill—Maen, in Sennen—Lesnewth 77

The Trevelgue Tumuli 80

III. CREMATION—Origin and relative age of the custom—the most usual mode of interment in Cornwall ... 90

The Menhirion, examples of in Cornwall—sometimes tomb stones over burnt interments—*e.g.*, Pridden Longstone—Trelew Longstone—Trenuggo Longstone—Tresvenneck Longstone 94

Tregiffian Barrow and Longstone 107

Of the various kinds of Tumuli met with in Cornwall—Cone-shaped Barrows—Bowl Barrows—Bell Barrows—Flat Barrows—Ring Barrows 111

Circles, divided into two classes, *(a)* of erect stones, *e.g.* Tregaseal, &c., &c., whose sepulchral *origin* is doubtful—*(b)* of contiguous stones, which latter are the Ring Barrows—*e.g.*, Goonorman—Botrea—Trescaw—and Wendron 120

Remarks on the selection of a spot for the burial—the ceremony of the interment—and the subsequent formation of the Barrow 137

	PAGE
Barrow on Trewavas Head	140
Remarks on the deposition of articles with the dead, and the practice of slave-killing	141
THE FICTILIA OF THE TUMULI—divided into three classes—*Vase-shaped Urns*—*Cylindrical Urns*—and *Miniature Urns*	144
EXPLORATIONS AND DISCOVERIES IN THE TUMULI—The 'One-Barrow'—Barrows at Lanyon—Veryan Beacon—Samson, Scilly—Withiel—Trelowarren—Chikarn—Bosavern Ros—Gwythian—Durval—Trewinard—Kerris—Goldvadnek—Karnmenelez—Perran Sands—St. Mary's, Scilly—Karn, Morvah—Miscellaneous—St. Austell Downs—Pelynt—Newquay—Glen Dorgal—Trevelgue Cliff-Castle—Place—Gerrans—Portscatha—Trevello Karn—Trannack—Conquer Downs—Brane Common—Boleit *(with traditions of a battle field at)*—Boscawen-ûn—Clahar Garden—Penquite—Sennen—Tredinney—Angrowse, 1st barrow at—2nd ditto—Pradanack—Denzell Downs—Morvah-Hill	152
THE AGE OF THE MONUMENTS—late Roman coins found in Cornwall—state of the country during the Romano-British period—hut-circles referable to this period—the tumuli are the sepulchres of the dwellers in the huts—the Towednack Cromlech—Chywoone Cromlech—notes on Flint Chips—Conclusion	253
ADDENDA.—*(a)* Sepulchral Monuments in Meneage—*(b)* Boskednan Circle and Barrow—*(c)* Barrows near Bosporthennis, Zennor	275

Nænia Cornubiæ.

"Grey stones on many a gloomy mountain mark
Where sleep the giant warriors of the West."
* * * * * * * *
"Perchance we now on dust of heroes tread,
Who, as in life, in death have made the heath their bed."

The Vale of Lanherne.

RCHÆOLOGY, whatever may be its pretensions to be called a separate science, can never fail to be of the greatest value when it seeks to rest the vapoury superstructure of theory or tradition upon the firm basis of observed fact. The geologist may have puzzled himself into the conclusion that for his purposes time is no object; but with the Antiquary the first care must always be to affix, where he sees a possibility of so doing, an approximate date, at

least, to each individual object that comes under his notice. It is in his ability to do this, that, in the popular point of view, the magic of his spell resides; and the first question of the labourer on discovering a relic is always the same: "When was it put here?" The "by whom," and "for what purpose" being as invariably subsequent.

But, the almost inevitable tendency of every writer, who has once possessed his mind of a spontaneous or favoured theory, is to make every circumstance which may subsequently occur to him, either fit in with his view, or if he cannot do this, to discard it as unworthy of his serious attention. The more firmly rooted the notion becomes, the more readily will doubtful points be explained away, and the less alive will he be to the possibility of their existence at all.

From any such tendency it is hoped that this essay will be found entirely free. It is true that in the few pages at the end, a conclusion has been arrived at, and consequently an opinion expressed as to the date of the monuments. This opinion, however, has been formed simply on the evidence of the tumuli themselves; and as it is in direct opposition to the views expressed by several eminent modern writers on the subject, the author begs the favourable consideration of a proposition forced, as it were, upon him by his own discoveries; and therefore put forth with the utmost deference to the judgment of those, whose experience has exceeded his own.

Of all the various ranges of study pursued in the present day, that of Antiquities is the one of all others in which theory, or idle speculation, should be most carefully avoided; yet, strange to say, it is the very one in which it has always been most freely indulged. Inductive evidence is all it has a right to; the spade is the only true needle to guide its course. If sufficient evidence of this kind can be gained to establish a point, well and good; but, as a recent writer very truly says, let the reasoning be "from the known to the unknown," never the reverse.

Thus, the reader will observe that throughout this little volume no stress is laid upon the hypothetical distinctions drawn between Stone, Bronze, and Iron Periods. This is simply because, as regards the Cornish *sepulchral* relics at least, no such line of demarcation seems admissible. Not that the county Museums are by any means destitute of relics, which, taken individually, without regard to where or in what company they were found, would at once be ascribed to one of the two first of these periods. For instance, two beautifully polished stone celts, one of jade or chert, and the other of green marble, were found respectively on the North Coast of Devon, and in a quarry at Falmouth, and are deposited in the

Truro Museum. Dr. Borlase, also, gives an engraving of a neatly formed flint axe-head, in his Antiquities of Cornwall; and a very similar one, found in a valley below St. Columb Minor, is in the possession of Mr. Hoblyn, of Fir Hill. These, and many others, would doubtless be set down, and perhaps rightly so, by modern Archæologists to what is termed the Neolithic, or ground-stone age; but, in the present instance, the reader is saved from speculating further on this subject, by the fact that no similar ones have as yet occurred in connection with those sepulchral interments, with which alone this volume is concerned.

Flints of a much ruder class, as will appear in the sequel, *have* been taken from Cornish barrows, but these have occurred side by side with pottery, bearing comparison with fictilia of a later date than that assigned to the most recent portion of the Age of Stone.

Again, with regard to Bronze: Celts of this metal, of all shapes, even the rarest, have been found in almost every quarter of the county, not unfrequently in connection with leaf-shaped spear and arrow heads, and very often in ancient mine workings. Instances, there are, where these weapons *have* occurred in connection with sepulchral remains, and these will be mentioned in their right place. But here again the theory of the Ages receives a shock. For instance, the author, for some time, believed that bronze daggers, similar to the one here engraved, belonged to a time considerably subsequent to that of the celts.

BRONZE DAGGER FOUND WITH A CELT AT BENALLECK, NEAR PAR. Length 16 inches. From a drawing by the late Canon Rogers.

Some half-dozen instances of the appearance of these daggers side by side with urns of the chevron pattern, such as have been found with late Roman coins, led him at first to this conclusion. The above drawing, however, shows one of these daggers found in *close* proximity to a celt,[1] similar to the one from Godolphin figured at page 30. Added to this; there are authentic examples of Roman coins actually having been found *with* celts, both in the case of the Karnbrè specimens,[2] and also at Mopus. Here then is a difficulty for Mr. Worsaae. What if a few of his country-

---

[1] The "noscitur a socio" is a principle too lightly regarded by those on whom it forces a conclusion they do not like. In the case of Antiquities it is, if judiciously used, extremely valuable.

[2] For the former instance see Borlase 281, and also Hitchins and Drew, i, 199. For the latter see the MS. of the late Canon Rogers.

Dr. Borlase's testimony on this point seems really conclusive. "With these instruments," he says, meaning the Karnbrè celts, "were found several Roman coins, six of which came into my hands." He mentions three of them as those of (1) Antoninus, (2) Constantius, and (3) Severus Alexander.

men (antiquaries instead of pirates) would once more turn their prows to the now friendly shores of Danmonia? Would the solid entrenchments (of fact) be proof against them this time?

The truth is that the whole theory of these periods, applicable to certain localities perhaps, or useful for purposes of mild generalization, breaks down directly it is considered as universally inclusive, or is applied at random to individual instances.

It is true that Archæology is, in a measure, the Science of Transitions; but then it must be remembered that it deals with centuries of unmarked invention, as well as with unrecorded migrations of the human race.

Each new discovery must, therefore, stand on its own merits; and the Antiquary, in the course of his researches, must ever be ready to be taken by surprise, and never be astonished to find a pet notion rudely dashed to the ground by a stroke of the pickaxe, or a turn of the shovel. Never should he be ready to sacrifice a fact, merely because it is hard to explain, upon the altar of a much more indefensible theory; and should he, in exploring remains which he considers pre-historic, chance to light upon any object which would bring them within the pale of history, he should, before discarding it, ask himself fairly the question: "Why should not this monument belong to the same period to which I know this relic must be assigned?" "Time," as Sir Thomas Browne says, "antiquates antiquities;" but what right has the antiquary to usurp that office? Should he not rather strain a point to keep the object within range, than rush forward to plunge it for ever in the chaos which is said to have existed "in the days when the earth was young?"

As, however, the object of this essay is not to advocate this or that theory, but simply to afford Archæologists of every shade of opinion a complete and detailed account of each and every discovery, drawings have been made even of the most minute objects, such as chippings of flint, which, as they occurred near the interments, may be thought by some to throw a light on the subject. For the same reason all further comment on the age of the monuments is reserved until the end of the work.

Before proceeding to describe the Cornish tumuli, &c., it is necessary to say a word or two with regard to another theory, which still retains its hold on the popular mind, though scarcely on that of the *savans* of the nineteenth century.

Recent investigations have served to convince archæologists that, in order to form any adequate idea of the primitive sepulchral rites practised in these islands, they must not content themselves with exploring those monuments alone, which, as Dr. Wilson remarks, owe their origin to the small heap of earth thrown out of the grave, but must extend their investigations also to the greater portion of that megalithic series, still so intimately associated in the minds of most people with boughs of mistletoe, golden knives, and white-robed Druids.

It is hard to conceive how the quaint speculations of a few individuals, fresh from the classics of the eighteenth century, could ever have taken such deep root in the popular mind, as those have done which connect the Druids with monuments of this class. Grounded on no documentary evidence, and often teeming with the most absurd fancies, these theories had become a part of the national tradition of this country; and had they not been subjected to the withering glance of a nineteenth century critic,[1] might absolutely have insinuated themselves into history itself.

Cornwall possessed in Dr. Borlase almost the earliest, and perhaps the least fanciful, of the advocates of the Druid theory. A word or two therefore on the change which has taken place since his time, in the bearings of this subject, may not be inappropriate, before the hoary phantom is banished for ever from the shade of his "accustomed oak."

It must not be understood that there is any pre-

---

[1] Mr. Nash; author of the "Bards and Druids."

tence for dismissing the Druid from his *proper* place in the early pages of the British Annals. His strange creed, combining, as it did, a teaching similar to that of Pythagoras, with a ceremonial revolting even to Roman ideas of humanity, is equally a matter of history with the cruel massacre which stained the shores of his holy isle of Mona. Both facts are recorded by historians, whose authenticity is in point of fact beyond dispute. But, thanks to the masterly scholarship and indefatigable zeal of those gentlemen who of late years have made the Celtic records of their country their special study, other sources than the classics may with safety be appealed to for evidence of the existence of Druids. Dr. Todd, in his "Life of St. Patrick," remarks that "there is evidence that Druidism and its attendant superstitions were in existence (in Ireland) in the times of the second order of saints, and that a belief in the efficacy of such pagan rites still lingered amongst the people." The Druidism of St. Columba's day was, however, a very different thing from the system of barbarity practised under the guise of philosophy or religion, mentioned by the classic authors. The term "Druidæ" had now become synonymous with the Latin "Magi;" (as see Dr. Reeves' Adamnan's Life of St. Columba, p. 73, note); and Zeuss (Gram. Celt. i, 278,) quotes a gloss in the Irish MS. of St. Paul's epistles at Wurzburg, in which Jamnes and Mambres are styled "da druith ægeptaedi." Thus the Archon Basileus of the first century had in fact degenerated into the Simon Magus of the sixth, and St. Patrick himself maintained that his fate did not depend "on the voice of birds, nor on the roots of a knotted tree, nor on the noise of the clapping of hands, nor lots, nor sneezing, nor a boy, nor chance, nor women;" but, he adds, "Christ, the son of God, is *my* Druid." In the Irish additions to the Historia Britonum collated by Mr. Skene from the Books of Ballymote and Lecain (Chron. Picts and Scots, p. 31), is the following :—" Drostan, the Druid of the Cruthneach, *i.e.* the Picts, ordered that the milk of seven score white cows should be spilled when the battle should be fought." Further on in the same translation the epithet "demnach," demonlike, is applied to the Druids; and "Druidheacht," literally "Druid's feat or work," is rendered (in accordance with O'Donovan's O'Reilly) "necromancy." In the same author's translation of the Four Ancient Books of Wales the word occurs only four times, and then apparently in the sense of "soothsayer," as in the poem entitled the "Omen of Prydein the Great," (vol. i, p. 442), "Druids foretell what great things may happen." Taking these passages into consideration, a qualification must be added to the dictum of Mr. Nash, and it must be said "that the Druid extinguished by Paulinus in A.D. 58, had not been resuscitated," *in his ancient character at least,* " in the tenth century," but that in the meantime the few good qualities which he once possessed had been lost sight of in the miserable arts of sorcery, divination, and magic. The existence and relative status in society of the Druid being thus ascertained at each end, as it were, of the historic chain, the question arises, whether or not he has any title to those mysterious monuments which the scholarship of the last century, and the Ordinance Surveyors of the present, have vied with one another in making over to him.

Investigation, as was said before, taking the place of theory, has proved the greater part of these monuments sepulchral, and therefore presumably unconnected with any distinct religious observances; but many still remain, like unclaimed dividends in the bank of our national history, awaiting a claimant to appropriate them to himself. If in the Druid there exists indeed such a claimant, it can only be said that his title still remains not proven. It is true that there are instances where his name, or one so similar as to be strikingly misleading, seems to have been connected in very remote times with localities where megalithic remains are found;[1] and the " Glain nan Druidhe," or Druids' glass beads of Scotland, prove that such was also the case with respect to certain

---

[1] Caer Druidion, Stanton Drew, &c.

charms. The author, however, has not been able to discover any satisfactory instance in Cornwall where the application of the term to any place or object can reasonably be traced further back than to the appearance of Borlase's work in 1754, which, like many others about that period, became, in the absence of all real traditions, a convenient text book of local superstition.[1] But even such names, where they do exist, may be referred to the magician of the sixth century, with much more probability than to the genuine Druid of the first; and those weird stones, which, by their gigantic proportions, as well as by the romantic situations in which they are generally placed, naturally excite the idolatrous veneration of a superstitious people, would be the very spots chosen by the soothsayer as the most fit and proper places for the practice of his imposture. However this may be, and to what people or purposes such

---

[1] On this subject most kind communications have been received, both from Mr. Robert Hunt, F.R.S., author of "The Romances and Drolls of the West of England;" and from Mr. Bottrell, author of the "Traditions and Hearthside Stories of West Cornwall." Both these gentlemen, than whom none are more qualified to offer an opinion, agree in their verdict that the *name* "Druid" does not enter into any one single tradition, which can be ascribed to a date anterior to Borlase's Work. Mr. Bottrell's words are: "the Druids are not known to any west-country folk but those who have seen them in books or heard them from Antiquaries; nor do they occur in our folk-lore, although unusual names and expressions, of which the meaning is unknown, are found in several old stories. The word "Druid" is not found in any charms that I have heard, and I think I know all those in use, or that were used a century past by west-country charmers."

structures as Stonehenge, Abury, and Carnac, with their attendant holed stones, rocking stones, &c., will finally be assigned, are subjects which will be only incidentally adverted to here when the question of the origin of the circles comes under discussion. For the present, something more tangible may be obtained by the consideration of those monuments whose sepulchral character has been placed beyond a doubt.

Sir John Lubbock has summed up the characteristic features of the primitive sepulchre in the remark: "A complete burial place may be described as a dolmen, covered by a tumulus, and surrounded by a stone circle. Often, however, we have only the tumulus, sometimes only the dolmen, and sometimes only the circle." To this list if there be added "sometimes only two adjacent menhirs, and sometimes only the simple standing stone," under the one or the other head may be classed every mode of interment hitherto discovered in Cornwall.

Firstly, the Dolmen, or Cromlech.

So much has been surmised and written on the probable derivation of this word, that the subject is only here introduced for the sake of recording the fact that, whatever it may signify,[1] it was in use as a

---

[1] After all, the most appropriate and satisfactory derivation of 'Cromlech'

local name in Cornwall, as well as in Wales or Ireland. "Rescal Cromlegh" represents, in an ancient deed, one of the boundaries of the property belonging to the Deanery of St. Buryan; a tract of country, even at the present day, more full of megalithic remains than perhaps any other of like extent in the Duchy. Unfortunately, the spot cannot be now identified, where this Cromlech, if indeed it was one in the usual sense of the term, stood.

European Cromlechs are capable of division into three classes. 1. The dolmen, or "table-stone" proper, where, as Colonel Forbes Leslie remarks, "the vertical supporters of the tabular stone are columnar," and cannot be said to *enclose* a space. 2. The Larger Kist Vaen, or stone chest, where, as the name implies, " the vertical supports are slabs ;" and, together with the covering stone, form a structure not unlike what children build with five cards. These were designed to hold the interment within the chamber, and were covered, sometimes very slightly,

---

seems to be found in the Irish '*crom*,' Welsh '*crum*,'="bent," hence "inclined over," (whence the Gaelic cromadh—a roof or vault, and M. Bullet's "ce qui enferme, ce qui couvre ;") and lech, "a stone." In slight confirmation of this idea, (which seems much more probable than that it means a "circle,") take a line from the Cornish "Origo Mundi," (2443,) where this same word '*crom*' appears as an epithet for rafters, the wood being "brás ha crom y ben goles"—"large and rounded (or vaulted) its lower side." The word would thus apply, like that of "Quoit," to the "covering stone" only, and not to the whole monument.

with conical, or other mounds. 3. Monuments, similar in structure to the last, but raised *over* the interment. These were merely cenotaphs, such as are frequently found in modern churchyards, not intended to contain the body, but to mark the spot, where the less pretencious grave was concealed below. Craig-Madden[1] in Stirlingshire, and many of the rude Irish cromlechs, are instances of this latter class; as well as the more prominent examples in Denmark and Norway,[2] and at Saulcieres[3] in France, where the kists actually occur on the *summits* of the tumuli. No instances of this latter class are extant in Cornwall.

Of these three classes, (and many subdivisions of them might be made, for each individual monument has some distinguishing characteristic of its own), the first, or "Dolmen proper," is comparatively of rare occurrence. In height it much exceeds the others, and the difficulty of its construction must have been proportionately greater. Three of the finest specimens of this class of cromlech are to be found respectively at Pentre Ifan,[4] in Pembrokeshire, Castle Wellan, in Ireland,[5] and Lanyon, in Cornwall. Caerwynen, in the latter county, is another instance of the

---

[1] Wilson's Prehist. Annals of Scotland. Edit. 1863, Vol. i, p. 93.
[2] Wormius. Mon. Dan. Liber primus. Hafniæ. 1643, p. 8.
[3] Waring's Monuments of Remote Ages, p. 26, pl. xxxi.
[4] Archæologia Cambrensis, 1865.
[5] Fergusson's Rude Stone Monuments, p. 45.

same mode of construction, and the ruder trilithons of the continent seem to belong to a like category. The form of these monuments in itself precludes the idea of the interment having taken place immediately beneath the covering stone, or of a tumulus having been raised over them; for, had such been the case, the débris of the mound must inevitably have forced its way at once into the chamber, the very result which, it is known, the builders of the kists were always so careful to guard against. Dr. Wilson, therefore, regards monuments of this kind as "the true cromlechs," not in themselves subterranean chambers, but memorial structures raised over the grave. Such was the design in the case of one at least of these,—that at Lanyon, in the parish of Madron, the finest and in all probability the most primitive[1] of our Cornish pre-historic remains.

LANYON CROMLECH.

This monument, as will be seen from the accompanying engraving taken from Borlase's Cornwall,[2]

---

[1] Since the above was written, Dr. Fergusson's work on Rude Stone Monuments, has made its appearance. With regard to the antiquity of these "tripod dolmens" he expresses the contrary opinion, and believes them to be the more modern of the two classes. Though bowing to so high an authority, the author must quote Dr. Fergusson's words (p. 46) that "with our limited knowledge it is hardly safe to insist on this."

[2] The accuracy of the dimensions given in Borlase is fully borne out by a drawing of the same monument made by the late Canon Rogers, in 1797, eighteen years before its fall.

consisted, until its fall in the year 1815, of three slim pillars of unhewn granite, supporting on their summits a horizontal stone, at a sufficient height from

LANYON CROMLECH, PREVIOUS TO ITS FALL. ELEVATION.
From Dr. Borlase's Antiquities of Cornwall.

the ground to permit a man mounted on horseback to sit under it. The cap stone, or "quoit," as it is

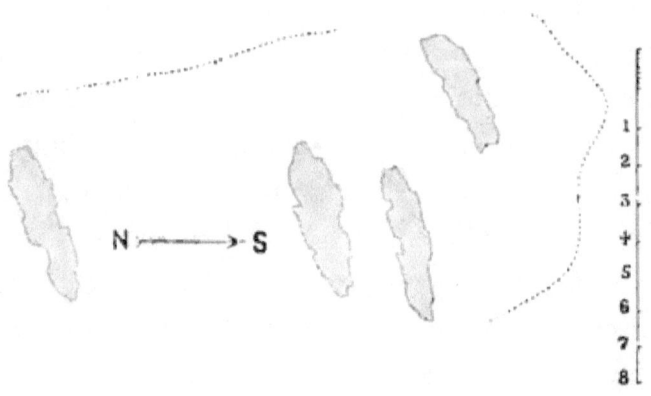

THE SAME. GROUND PLAN.

termed in Cornwall, measured, (before a piece was broken off it), 47 feet in circumference, and averaged

20 inches thick. Viewed from the opposite hill, for it stands on high ground, the whole structure may not, even in its present stunted form,[1] be inaptly compared to a three-legged milking-stool. About the middle of the last century, a dream induced the owner of the property to dig beneath it, and directly under the "quoit" a simple grave was discovered, cut in the natural soil, without side stones or covering. At the depth of six feet the explorers reached the bottom; but unfortunately the other dimensions are not recorded. Although this pit was carefully searched on that occasion, and subsequently rifled more than once, Dr. Borlase assures us that nothing was found "more than ordinary." From this discovery, it seems quite clear that inhumation was the mode of burial practised in this case; for had cremation taken place, ashes, or at all events strata of burnt earth, would have been found; and it is only on the supposition that the corpse was laid unprotected in the porous ground, without any imperishable articles accompanying it, that the total absence of relics in the grave can be at all accounted for. Had the length of the cavity been recorded, some inference might have been formed as to the position in which the body was placed; that is,

---

[1] It was set up again in 1824, but several of the stones had been broken, and one of the supporters bears marks of recent cleavage. At present a person must stoop to pass under it.

whether it was extended at full length, or contracted, with the knees bent up towards the chin. Trivial as such a distinction may at first sight appear, it is just one of those points which, if carefully followed up, may one day become valuable to the ethnologist in distinguishing the lines of demarcation to be drawn between the various races or tribes inhabiting this country in the primitive era.

The different modes of disposing of the body, which meet the explorers of the early sarcophagi of Great Britain, are three in number. Interments have either been placed in the ground *whole*, or they have been reduced to ashes by (1) *cremation*. Those bodies which have been buried in their entirety are either (2) *extended* or (3) *contracted*. Leaving the subject of cremation for a future page, it may be remarked with reference to the practice of inhumation, that throughout the North of England it is by far the most common mode of burial; and that in England generally the contracted form of it has been found to have prevailed very largely over the extended. Thus the Rev. Canon Greenwell, in a letter dated the 12th of December, 1871, informs the author that "out of above 200 interments of what may be considered pre-Roman times," he has only found " a single instance where the body had been buried in an extended position." So much for the North.

Coming further South the combined researches of Sir R. C. Hoare and Thomas Bateman, Esq., tabulated by Sir John Lubbock, show that out of some 500 interments explored with care, only thirty-seven were extended, while 112 were contracted, the rest being burnt.

In Cornwall a marked difference is observable. Well authenticated instances of inhumation at all are extremely rare. Among these, only two or three examples of the extended position actually occur; but the not-uncommon occurrence of empty long graves, whether cut in the hard soil or walled with stones, affords a strong presumption that, had they not been rifled, a similar mode of interment might have been discovered in them. Of the contracted position, as will be seen hereafter, only one really authentic instance can be cited.

As to the relative ages of these two modes of sepulture, it would be hard to make even an approximate guess. Dr. Fergusson, speaks of Canon Greenwell's contracted discoveries as " really pre-historic," and he is probably right. But a pre-disposition, in favor of the simplicity and appropriateness of our present custom, has led many to the conclusion that the extended mode would more naturally have suggested itself to man in the earliest stages of civilized life. Should this latter notion be adopted, it must not be overlooked that the return to the primitive custom, in Christian times, must always induce the doubt whether graves of this description may not belong to a much more recent period.

As in the case of Lanyon, an empty earth-cut grave has been mentioned in connection with megalithic remains, it may not be amiss, before passing on to describe a second "tripod" Cromlech, to notice two other instances where a similar grave has been found. In each of these cases, the monument has consisted of two pillars of unhewn granite placed at no great distance apart. Graves adorned in this manner are the common property of all ages and all religions. Their history was just as much out of remembrance in the days of Homer, as it is now:—

$$\Lambda\tilde{\alpha}\varepsilon\ \delta\grave{\varepsilon}\ \tau\tilde{o}\upsilon\ \dot{\varepsilon}\kappa\acute{\alpha}\tau\varepsilon\rho\theta\varepsilon\upsilon\ \dot{\varepsilon}\upsilon\eta\rho\acute{\varepsilon}\delta\alpha\tau\alpha\iota\ \delta\acute{\upsilon}o\ \lambda\varepsilon\upsilon\kappa\grave{\omega},$$
$$\text{῍Η τευ σῆμα βροτοῖο πάλαι κατατεθνηῶτος.}^{1}$$

A sketch in the "Univers Pittoresque" of two rude stones in Corsica, might serve as an adequate representation of the Cornish specimens; and the Giant's Grave at Penrith Churchyard, in Cumberland,[2] is doubtless one of the earliest instances of the gradual introduction of the head-stone and foot-

---

[1] Homer's Iliad, lib. xxiii. 329.
 Mr. Wright translates the pasage:—
   "On either side"
  "rise two white stones set there"
 "To mark the tomb of some one long since dead."
[2] Higgins' Celtic Druids, p. 148.

stone so commonly set up by Christian[1] mourners of the present day.

Two monuments of this kind are extant in Cornwall. They are situated within a mile or two of each other, and of the Lanyon Cromlech, and both have been explored, the first by Dr. Borlase in the year 1752, and the second by the author in 1871.

The former[2] is situated in a field sloping towards the west, on the estate of Trewren, in the parish of Madron. The respective heights of the two rough pillars in this case are five and six feet above ground, and the distance between them ten feet. They point in a direction E. by N., and W. by S. "Upon searching the ground between these two stones the diggers presently found a pit six feet six long, two feet nine wide, and four feet six deep; near the bottom it was full of black greasy earth, but no bone to be seen. This grave came close to the Westernmost and largest stone, next to which, I imagine, the head of the interred lay. The Christians in some parts buried in this manner, but in compliance, as it is to be imagined, with a more ancient Pagan custom."[3] The author of these pages was fortunate enough to be present some few years since, when this

---

[1] "The Monk, O'Gorgon, is buried near to the Chapel, and there is a Stone five Foot high at each End of this Grave." Martin, Isles of Skie, p. 167.
[2] See elevation and ground plan in Borlase's Antiquities, p. 146, pl. x.
[3] Borlase, Ant. of Corn., p. 187.

grave was re-opened by the late William Coulson, Esq., the owner of the land, when the above account was fully confirmed. The black soil in the grave is the peat natural to the country.

At Trigganeris, or Higher Drift, in the adjoining parish of Sancreed, there stands, on the top of the hill, another monument, evidently of the same description as the last. It consists, as in the former case, of a taller and a shorter pillar, the former nine feet in height, the latter seven feet four inches. The direction in which they lie is NNW. and SSE. During the excavation of a trench between these stones the author came upon the end of a cavity cut with much

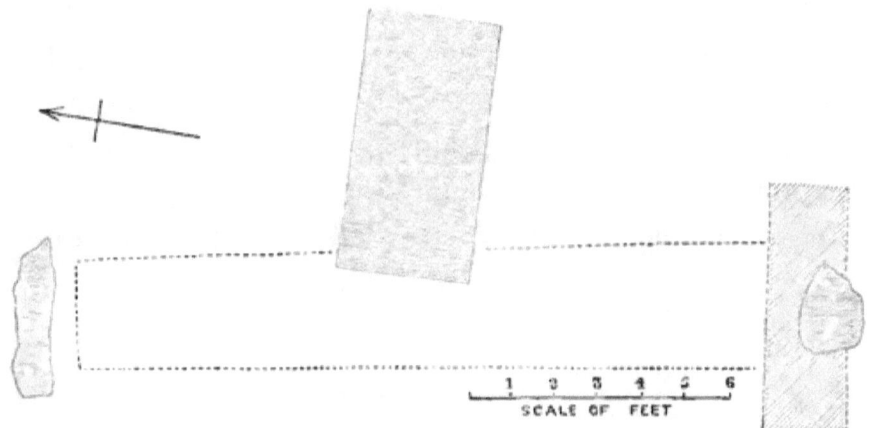

GROUND PLAN OF TRIGGANERIS STONES AND GRAVE.

precision in the hard natural clay, or, as the Cornish term it, "rabman." This proved to be a grave six feet long, three feet three broad, and about five deep, corresponding remarkably with the dimensions of that at Trewren. It lay, however, not lengthways between the pillars, but nearly at right angles to them, and completely out of the line, so that a tape stretched from the centre of the one to the centre of the other scarcely, if at all, passed through a corner of it. No flat stones were found in the grave, nor indeed anything but the fine disturbed sub-soil of the neighbourhood.[1]

Remarkable as is the attempt at orientation in both these cases, and in the latter especially, (for the Trigganeris grave lies nearly due East and West) it must still be noticed that in no respect do these pillars differ in character from the rudest of the menhirs, and the other members of the megalithic family; nor do they show any traces of the patterns and letters which distinguished the tombs of the primitive Christians. No remains or traditions of chapelries or oratories are extant in their vicinity, and if they are indeed to be ascribed to Christians at all, they form a striking link in the sepulchral history of that dark uncertain period.

CAERWYNEN CROMLECH.

After this digression it remains to glance at the one other instance of a "Cromlech proper" which

---

[1] Canon Greenwell remarks that "empty graves are not uncommon, and that it depends upon surrounding circumstances, whether the bones have decayed or not," he having "found them in all stages of decay."

Cornwall affords; before passing on to the more extensive subject of the Kist Vaens. This monument is situated in the centre of a sloping meadow on a tenement called Caerwynen, immediately opposite the front windows of the old family mansion of Pendarves. Similar to Lanyon Cromlech in its construction, it has also shared its fate, for it fell many years since; but was, as a labourer asserted who had assisted in the work, soon after replaced by the patriotic lady of the manor, in much the same position as before. Fortunately a drawing of it, by Borlase, (larger than that in his published work), is extant in his MS. collections, from which the accompanying engravings are taken.

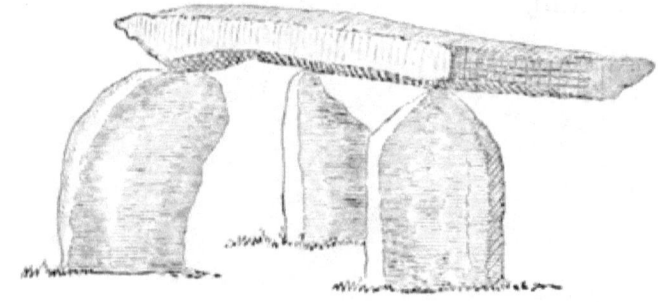

CAERWYNEN CROMLECH,
From a Drawing by Dr. Borlase.

The two supporters at the south-eastern end seem to have retained their original positions. They were, formerly, respectively 5 feet 1 inch, and 5 feet 2 inches above ground, and are still nearly the same height. The single pillar at the other side has been moved nearer the edge of the covering stone than in the above sketch; it measured 4 feet 11 inches high, but is now shorter. The covering slab, which, like the other stones, is granite, measures twelve feet by nine; one side, however, seems to have been broken in its fall. Some stones now standing on the north side, were placed there subsequently to the restoration. No pit was sunk beneath it, nor has it ever been explored, and there are no remains of a tumulus under or around it. If explored, (which would be in its present state a dangerous operation), it is highly probable that a grave similar to that at Lanyon would be found, the area between the supporters being formerly seven feet long, by about five broad, though now something more.

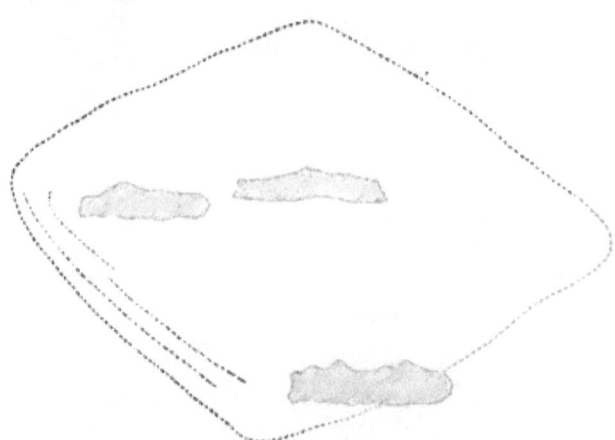

GROUND PLAN OF CAERWYNEN CROMLECH.
From a Drawing by Dr. Borlase.

A fallen Cromlech which may have possibly belonged to the "tripod" class, is to be found near

Helmen Tor, in the parish of Lanlivery. A drawing of this will be found in Blight's "Crosses of East Cornwall," p. 131.

The distinction between "the Cromlech proper," such as that just described, and the "Larger Kist Vaen" has been already noticed. In proceeding to consider this latter class it will be found that it comprises every other monument of the kind still extant in Cornwall.

The idea of building a habitation for the dead owes its origin to the most primitive times; and may be regarded as one of the earliest conceptions of the mind of man. It belongs to a state of society when death, considered as a total extinction or annihilation, was by no means fully realized ;[1] nor, on the other hand, had the future life yet been defined as a matter of certitude or religious contemplation. Thus, the four walls and roof rose around and covered the corpse, the five plain slabs presenting the most ready, as well as the most substantial model of the dwelling house, and affording the first requisite in domestic architecture, namely:—protection from external adverse circumstances. Thus was formed the true "Beth" or "Bedd," the "Bod" or "Bos" of the

---

[1] In some of the Indian, and the Circassian dolmens, a hole is bored in one of the side-stones, supposed to be indented for the reception of food for the occupant of the tomb.

Cornu-Britons; firstly, the home of the living, and secondly, the οἶκος τῶν νεκρῶν — the chamber of the dead. Not that any of our British Cromlechs have actually *served* the former purpose, like the Gangrabben of Scandinavia, or the hovels of those modern savages, who, on the death of the tenant, immediately convert his temporary holding into a fee-simple for ever by blocking up the entrance: but still, it is more than probable that the idea was the same throughout, and that the Kist Vaen was in its origin simply a contracted or miniature representation of the class of residence occupied by the deceased during life. This idea is supported in great measure by a comparison of the rude masonry displayed in these structures, (the extended or passage ones particularly), with that of the huts and underground chambers which so frequently occur in their immediate vicinity. It must, however, be observed that this style of architecture, if indeed it can be called such, belongs to nearly every inhabited district in the world; everywhere in fact, where slabs of granite or flag stones afford materials ready at hand for the execution of so simple a design. That edifices so constructed are of a most primitive type must at once be clear to all who are willing to admit that, in the absence of reliable evidence, simplicity of design only signifies priority of construction. The comparison between man in his primitive state and children who act by the light of nature alone, has been often made: and the author will only add, that on a Cornish goose green, in the midst of the hamlet or "town place," he has more than once watched the formation of a group of dolmens, which, if only magnified, would rival those of the Khasias, or any other tribe of dolmen-builders in ancient or modern times. Indeed, the masonry displayed in the Larger Kist Vaen is peculiarly characteristic of man in his primeval or infantine state; and thus it seems that, by using a term such as "dolmen-builders," we cannot draw a line round any particular century, nation, or locality. It was the sepulchre alike of the early inhabitants of Malabar and of India, of Northern Africa, as well as of Western Europe, Denmark, Norway, and Sweden. Drawings and descriptions are continually brought home, of Cromlechs, which, with a very few characteristic differences, resemble so strangely those of Europe, that one might fancy they belonged not to any foreign clime, but to our own native hills. But while European writers are wondering at the universality of this mode of burial throughout so many widely distant countries of the globe, and are being startled by the fact that there are actually tribes in India who are erecting these very identical structures while they are writing and speculating, let them ask themselves the question, 'Are they so perfectly certain that they are not "dolmen-builders" themselves?' May there not be those who can see, not only in the Altar-tomb of the Romans, or the sarcophagus of the Middle Ages, but in the square cenotaph of our modern churchyard, the lineal descendant of the Pagan Kist Vaen? To make the chain complete, examples are not wanting of a transition period, which it would be most interesting to follow up. Many instances might be quoted of tombs of this class found in close proximity to early Christian edifices; and Dr. Petrie in especial has left us the record of one, at least, still standing near a ruined church in the island of Ardoilen. But to come to more recent times: Suppose for an instant that a native Khasian antiquary, (if such a fellow could be found), interested in the comparative ethnology of his race, were to visit Great Britain: Suppose him taken to a grave yard, say, in a slate district, where the square five-slab tombs abound, and would he not return to his native countrymen with the news that he had found a "group" of as genuine "dolmen-builders" as they themselves? It seems, therefore, only fair to conclude, that this primitive dwelling of the dead, deriving its origin to all appearance from the latent superstition of the earliest ages, subsequently received, with the spread of civilization, the sanction of custom and the protection of religion; and that even in its pristine form it has not yet disappeared from among the number of those monuments which adorn, or too often disfigure, our modern English churchyards.

It may be laid down as a general rule, which recent investigation has made almost universal,[1] that all the larger Kist Vaens, or Cromlechs of the second class were designed to contain the remains of the deceased *unburnt*. Professor Nillson,[2] remarking on the *dös*, or Scandinavian Cromlech, says, that it was "erected in order to contain *one* body only, which was always placed in a sitting posture." This, however, is not so invariably the case in other countries. At De Tus, in Guernsey, for example, Mr. Lukis[3] found two skeletons in the same kist, and a like number were taken from the Phœnix Park[4] Cromlech, at Dublin. In both these cases the bodies were contracted; but that the extended mode of inhumation was *never* practised in the larger Kist Vaens is by no means certain; and, with regard to those which are now empty, it seems only reasonable to suppose, that where the chamber is sufficiently long to contain an extended interment, the body was placed in that position; while, in the cases where it is too small to admit of such being the case, a sitting,

---

[1] An exception to this rule, in the case of a Cornish Cromlech, will be found at page   , but this may be a secondary interment.
[2] "Primitive Inhabitants of Scandinavia," translated by Sir John Lubbock, p. 159.
[3] Journal of the Archæological Association, vol. 1, p. 27.
[4] See Mr. Wakeman's admirable little "Handbook of Irish Antiquities," p. 9.

kneeling, or other contracted posture was resorted to. In Cornwall, the length of the Larger Kists averages from 10 feet to 6 feet; so that in each case a body might have been interred at full length. The one which will be first noticed, viz., that at Pawton, in the parish of St. Breock, seems more especially to point to this mode of sepulture.

PAWTON CROMLECH, FROM A SKETCH BY THE AUTHOR.

This monument is situated on high ground in the centre of a field immediately above the picturesque valley and ancient ecclesiastical establishment of Pawton.

The accompanying sketch, taken by the author a few months since, will, perhaps, convey some slight idea of the structure. The stones which form the grave are eight in number, but the covering stone itself rests on only three of them. They are still more than half buried in the tumulus which formerly, no doubt, covered the whole. This was of an oval shape, and upwards of sixty feet in length. The grave itself is seven feet long; and, but for a stone which has been inserted at one end, would be a foot and a half longer. This stone is probably a prop to support the one on which that end of the capstone rests. The width of the grave is two feet at one end, and three and a half at the other: it is at present five feet deep, though it may in all probability be several feet deeper. The sparry stone which forms the covering is thirteen feet in length, by seven in breadth; and, as a labourer informed me that a piece (marked A, in the accompanying plan,) had been broken off from it, the length may be increased by several feet. In thickness the covering stone is uniformly two feet six.

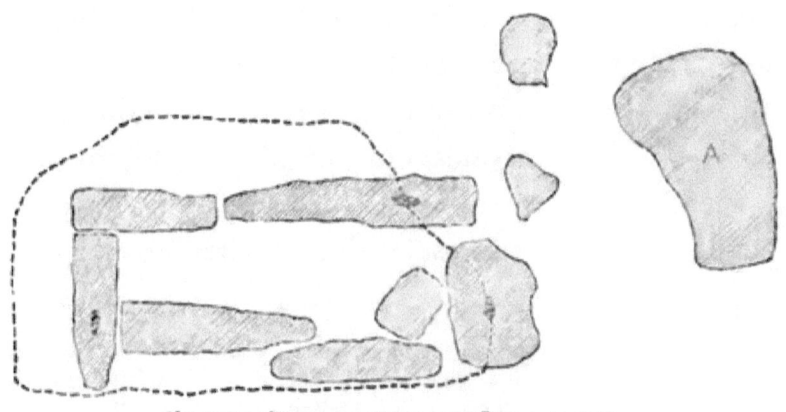

GROUND PLAN OF PAWTON CROMLECH [1].

---

[1] The dark spots in the plan represent the points of contact between the sides, and roofing stone.

From the shape and size of the kist in this case, there can be no doubt that it was constructed to contain a body at full length; and although, as was before noticed, interments in that position are so very rare in other parts of England, there *are* other instances (though few and far between) of similar graves in Cornwall, to prove that this mode of burial was not by any means unknown in that district. In several cases the author has particularly noticed that the grave is too narrow to admit of the body being contracted at all, and in more than one case a skeleton[1] extended has actually been found. Two or three of these long walled graves may here be described.

STONE GRAVES.

On the very top of the southernmost of the two hills which form the island of Sampson, Scilly, lie four or five narrow trenches, formed by long side-stones of granite, and in one or two cases still partly covered in by flat ones on the top. They at first appear like large drains or bolts, but on a closer inspection it may be observed that circular cairns of

---

[1] Carew, (Edit. 1, 1602, p. 159.) gives the following account of a skeleton, the position of which is unfortunately omitted. "Not farre from the lands ende, there is a little village called Trebegean, in English, the towne of the Giants grave: neere whereunto and within memory (as I have been informed) certayne workemen searching for Tynne, discovered a long square vault, which contayned the bones of an excessive bigge carkas, and verified this Etimology of the name."

stone have been raised round them, and that stones on edge have been placed at the end of each. In length these graves average seven feet, and in breadth two feet, or something less. A Kist-Vaen which was opened on the Northern side of the same island was found to contain calcined bones and a flint flake; this grave, however, was nearly square, and will be more fully described when the subject of cremation is under discussion.

In the MSS. of Dr. Borlase[1] is the following: "As you ride down to see the farthest projection of this (the Land's End) promontory, lye a few stones set in order, enclosing an oblong square about six foot long and three foot wide." On searching this spot a few months since, the author discovered this, or more probably another similar grave, not quite three feet wide by eight feet in length. Over this a labourer remembers seeing part of a covering stone, recently carried away.

Mr. Cotton[2] found in the most northern barrow on Botrea Hill, in the parish of Sancreed, on the 26th of September, 1826, "the remains of a Kist Vaen or stone grave, consisting of two large stones, set up edgeways, in a line with each other, about fifteen inches in height, and 6 feet 6 inches in length:

---

[1] Parochial Memoranda, p. 3.
[2] "Illustrations of Stone Circles," &c., "in the West of Cornwall," p. 39.

another stone (2 feet 8 inches long and overlapping the former,) was placed at right angles with these, and formed one end of the grave." In turning over the black earth with which this grave was filled, two flint arrow heads were found, "barbed and sharp pointed;" they were one inch and a half in length, by ⅞ths of an inch in breadth.

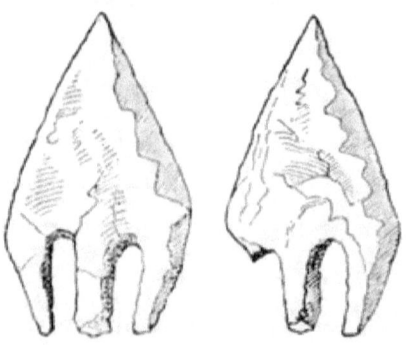

ARROW HEADS FROM BOTREA.
From Drawings by Mr. Cotton.

About the year 1748, the easternmost of three barrows at Bosavern Rôs, in the parish of St. Just, was opened, and in it, as Dr. Borlase has recorded, "was found the carcase of a man *laid at full length*; a long stone on each side, and one at each end on the edge, the cavity like a grave; the bones large sized; no stone covering the body.".[1]

But stone graves, such as these, have not been always so unproductive. The most curious and valu-

---

[1] "Ant. of Cornwall," 2 edit. p. 235.

able find hitherto made in any Cornish barrow, was brought to light in the year 1818, in a long grave under a stone cairn near the Cheesewring, in the parish of Linkinhorne.

A pile of stones, about thirty yards in diameter, covered an oblong cavity, eight feet long, three-and-a-half feet broad, and three feet high. Each of the sides of this grave was formed of three stones set on edge; one stone placed in the same manner closed each end; a long flat stone lay at the bottom of the cell, and a tenth stone formed the cover of the whole. Along the floor lay "the remains of a skeleton *extended*." Near the breast stood an earthen pot, and within[1] it a golden cup. A flat stone, sixteen inches square, leaning diagonally against the western side of the Kist, *covered* and protected these vessels.[2]

The earthenware vessel was broken in removing it, but "the fragments exhibited the usual incised ornamentation of the early British pottery."

Other relics were found in the same tomb, but are unfortunately mislaid—they comprised a small piece of ornamental earthenware; a bronze spear-head, ten inches long; something like a metallic rivet;[3] pieces of ivory, and a few glass beads.

---

[1] Such was the opinion of the workmen who found it.
[2] The vault lay N.N.E. and S.S.W.
[3] This dagger and rivet are probably of the same kind as that figured at page 4, found at Benallack, near Par. Several others will be mentioned in

It is to Sir Edward Smirke that the Antiquarian world is indebted for the re-discovery of the gold cup, and for the publication, in the Archæological Journal, of a most interesting account of it. Further particulars respecting it may be gained from a MS. letter by W. T. P. Shortt, Esq., of Exeter, to Dr. Wilson, extracts from which are to be found in the 'Pre-historic Annals of Scotland.'

GOLD CUP, FOUND NEAR THE CHEESEWRING.
From a Drawing by Sir Edward Smirke.

these pages. One is engraved by Borlase in the Ant. of Cornwall. It may be here noticed that:—

(1) The gold lunulæ, from Harlyn, were found *with a celt*.
(2) The gold cup, here mentioned, was found *with a rivetted bronze dagger*.
(3) A rivetted bronze dagger was found at Benallack *with a celt*.

Although these premises are not very satisfactory, still they may afford some slight evidence that these objects belonged to one and the same people, and perhaps to one and the same period.

The gold cup, of which a woodcut is here given, is three-and-a-quarter inches high; three-and-three-eights inches in diameter at the mouth; the handle measures one-and-a-half inches long, by seven-eighths of an inch in width. The weight is 2 oz. 10 dwts., and the bullion value, £10. The handle is slightly crushed, but is attached to the cup by six little rivets, secured by small lozenge-shaped nuts or collars.

The cup is terminated at the bottom by a round knob; and, as the handle is "only fit for means of suspension," Sir Edward judges that it was never intended to stand upright at all.

The corrugated pattern, or horizontal undulations on the surface of the cup, although extremely curious, are by no means unique. Concentric rings ranged round a boss formed, as is well known, the ordinary design for shields of beaten bronze. Doubtless these undulations added considerably to the defensible qualities and durability of the weapon in sustaining or warding off a blow. When applied to such an article as a cup, they may have afforded, as Sir Edward Smirke suggests, "some constructive advantage."[1]

Little vessels of clay, and even of amber,[2] with

---

[1] Messrs. Garrard, who examined and weighed the cup, considered that one "of the same material, might be produced, without difficulty, out of a single flat lamina of thin gold, hammered or beaten into a similar form."

[2] An amber vessel from Hove, near Brighton, much resembled this cup. With it was found "a bronze blade."

diminutive handles attached, are among the curiosities which have rewarded and puzzled the British barrow-digger; gold cups, however, though found in Denmark, are extremely rare, and Mr. Way gives it, as his opinion, that "none of a like description to this one have occurred among the numerous objects of gold found in Great Britain." Instances there are of personal ornaments formed of the same precious metal, and surrounded by the same corrugated pattern. One found in Lincolnshire, were it not that it is an armlet, would be a counterpart of the cup. Another, a bracelet from Camuston, Angus, was taken from a kist containing a skeleton, immediately beneath the shadow of an erect sculptured cross. With this latter was an urn, ornamented with the usual zigzag; and tradition marked the spot as the grave of a Dane, slain by Malcolm II. at the close of the VIIth century.[1]

It is a remarkable fact, that before this cup was found, there was a tradition in the neighbourhood of a "golden boat"[2] having been dug up in a stone cairn near the Cheesewring. When, a few months since, the author visited the ground, he found that all the cairns for miles round had been rifled by

---

[1] For these interesting comparisons the author is indebted to Mr. Way's supplementary notes to Sir E. Smirke's paper.

[2] Compare the tradition of a "golden boat" buried at Veryan beacon. Infra page.

treasure-seekers, who had doubtless heard of one of these two finds. On the brow of the downs rising to Sharp Tor are three large cairns, seemingly built round with some care, and immediately below them a large quantity of ruined British huts. Caradon Hill is covered with barrows and cairns, the largest of which is on the southern brow. All, however, have been searched.

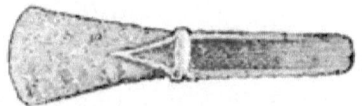

CELT FROM GODOLPHIN MINE.

The celt here figured is copied from the unpublished sketches of Cornish Antiquities made by the late Canon Rogers. The note accompanying it states that it was found, "with many others, *in a coffin* at Godolphin Mine, probably between 1740 and 1750." There seems little doubt but that this coffin was a stone kist, of the elongated shape, such as have just been described. Another celt, found in close proximity to a human skeleton, and described as of yellow metal, was dug up in the year 1790, twenty-six feet under the surface, in Carnon Stream-works. No kist is mentioned in this case.

Having digressed from the subject of the Cromlechs, in order to notice those smaller quadrated graves which, from their size and shape, seem, like that at Pawton, to have been intended for a body at full length, it is now time to return to the subject of the Kist-Vaen proper. Although, in every instance, the chamber of the Cornish Cromlech is sufficiently long to allow of an extended interment, yet those now to be noticed do not seem to suggest so pointedly as the long graves, that such was the case. The Kist Vaen proper is much wider and more lofty in proportion to its length, and would, indeed, easily contain any number of bodies placed in almost any posture whatever. In the only instance, however, where one of these kists has been disinterred from its surrounding tumulus in modern times, a *single* skeleton has been found, as the primary interment, showing that, in this case at least, the opinion of Professor Nillson, that such structures contained only one body, holds good in reference to the Cornish Cromlech, as well as to the Scandinavian *döss*.

LOWER LANYON CROMLECH.

The monument referred to is, curiously enough, situated on the same estate as the one lately described, namely, at Lanyon, in the parish of Madron; and is quite as good a specimen of the "Kist" type, as the former one was of the "Cromlech proper."

Two stones are all that now remain, viz., the covering stone, and one of the supporters; the others having been split up and carried away for building. A very rough sketch of this Cromlech, when perfect, will be found in Mr. Cotton's Illustrations of Antiquities in Cornwall, page 37; and the following notice of its discovery is preserved in the Archæologia, Vol. xiv, page 228.

"The gentleman who owns the estate of Lanyon, happening to be overtaken by a shower of rain in walking through his fields, took shelter behind a bank of earth and stones, and remarking that the earth was rich, he thought it might be useful for a compost. Accordingly, he sent his servants soon after to carry it off, when, having removed near a hundred cart loads, they observed the supporters of a Cromlêh, from which the coverstone was slipped off on the south side, but still leaning against them. These supporters include a rectangular space open only at the north end, their dimensions being of a very extraordinary size, viz., that forming the eastern side ten feet and a half long, that on the west nine feet, with a small one added to complete the length of the other side, and the stone shutting up the south end about five feet wide. The cover-stone is about thirteen feet and a half, by ten feet and a half." "As soon as the gentleman observed it to be a Cromlêh, he ordered his men to dig under it, where they soon found a broken urn with many ashes, and going deeper they took up about half of a skull, the thigh bones, and most of the other bones of a human body, lying in a promiscuous state, and in such a disordered manner as fully proved that the grave had been opened before; and this is the more certain, because the flat stones which formed the grave, or what Dr. Borlase calls the Kist Vaen, and a flat stone, about six feet long, which probably lay at the bottom, had all been removed out of their places." The measurements of the covering stone given in this account quite accord with those taken by the author a short time since. In thickness it averages from one foot six, to one foot nine inches. It may be reasonably doubted if, from its present position, this stone was ever raised to the place for which it had been intended. Had such been the case, the mound would no doubt have served to consolidate the whole fabric, and to keep it in its place; and its present appearance leads to the conclusion that the builders, in this case, were never able to complete the stupendous work which they had begun. One of the displaced stones mentioned above may, perhaps, have served as the covering stone of the interment, in the absence of the one designed for that purpose.

The accompanying plan is an attempted restoration of this Cromlech—(1st) from the stones as they now stand, (2nd) from the drawing by Mr. Colton, and (3rd) from the above account.

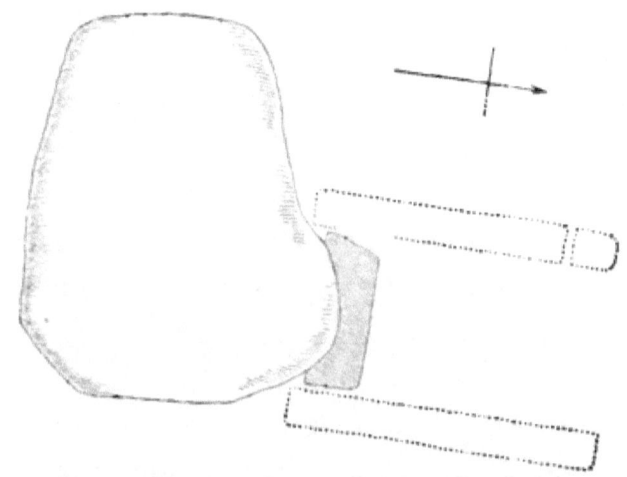

GROUND PLAN OF LOWER LANYON CROMLECH.

In leaving the subject of this interesting discovery, and in passing on to other monuments of a like nature, two things must be kept in mind; first, that here the reader has had an instance of a Cromlech actually *covered* by a mound; and secondly, that the primary interment within the kist consisted of a *single* body *unburnt*. These two facts are particularly worth remembering; since in the case of so few other monuments of the kind is anything left but the bare stones themselves to guide the work of elucidating their origin or purpose.

TRETHEVY CROMLECH.

The largest, though perhaps the least known of

the Cornish Cromlechs, is that of Trethevy, Trevethy, or, as the common people call it, Tredavy, in the parish of St. Clere. The earliest account of it is given by Norden, who, writing about the year 1610, says, "Trethevie, called in Latine *Casa gigantis*, a litle howse raysed of mightie stones, standing on a litle hill within a feilde, the forme hereunder expressed;" and accordingly there follows an original, but highly characteristic engraving of the monument. Two more recent notices of it appear respectively in the Journal of the Royal Institution of Cornwall, and the Report of the Penzance Natural History Society for the year 1850; in the former, the author being S. R. Pattison, Esq., F.G.S., and in the latter, E. H. Pedler, Esq. Of the two drawings here inserted, the first is from a photograph by Mr. Lobb, of Wade-

DRAWING OF TRETHEVY.

bridge, and the second from the accomplished pencil of J. T. Blight, Esq., F.S.A. From these two the reader may easily gather the chief peculiarities of the structure.

DRAWING OF TRETHEVY.

The monument consists of six upright stones, upon the upper edges of three of which, an oblong covering stone is at present diagonally resting. An eighth stone, probably at one time the supporter at the western extremity, has fallen lengthways along the kist, leaving that end open, and throwing the whole burden of supporting the horizontal stone upon two side-stones. These latter have consequently been forced out of the line at their base, and bowed inwards at their top, giving a circular or triagonal form to that end of the kist, seemingly by no means a part of the original plan. According to Mr. Pattison, "the fall of this western pillar caused the superincumbent stone in its descent to break off the upper portions of the side stones nearest to the fallen one, and thus it settled down in its present sloping condition." At its most elevated point the covering stone is thirteen feet from the ground, while at the other end, where it is most depressed, it is only seven-and-a-half. The longest diagonal is from S.W. to N.E., where it measures thirteen feet six; it is nine feet broad, and averages one foot in thickness.

But the most remarkable feature in this Cromlech, as it now stands, is the fine menhir which forms the principal and eastern supporter. In the choice of this stone, as well as in its erection, the greatest care and labour were evidently displayed. On the outer face it presents a smooth surface of finely-grained granite, while the squareness of the upper end, and the well coyned angles, give it almost the appearance of a wrought stone, and make it a most solid and substantial prop. It stands nearly ten feet in height above the small mound in which it is set up; and, to render it the more secure, another and ruder pillar, of nearly an equal height, is projected like a buttress against one side of it. The other four stones, which (two on each side) form the kist, are shorter than the eastern pillar by several feet. The fallen stone, once closing up the western end, seems, however, to have been considerably longer than these side ones; so that it is not improbable that this monument was originally a *trilithon*,[1] that is, that the covering stone was supported by two pillars only, one at each end of the grave. The interior of the kist was between nine and ten feet long, and from five feet six to six feet six broad. A pit in the centre shows that the stones rest, not on the mound, but on the natural surface of the ground beneath; so that the pile of earth and stones now lying round them must have been subsequently heaped there, but to what height it is impossible to say.

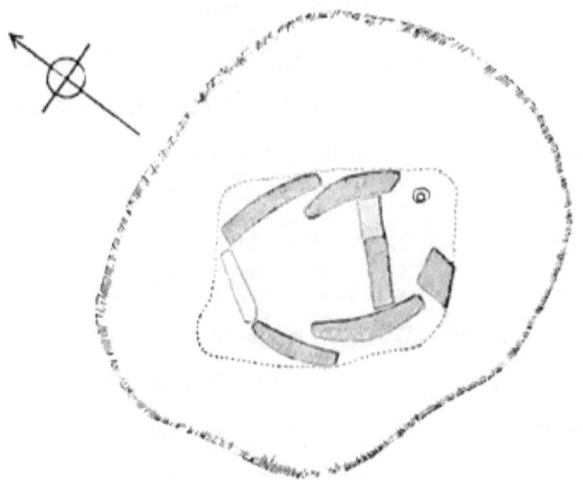

GROUND PLAN OF TRETHEVY.

There still remain two other features to be noticed in this Cromlech, since they have given rise to a considerable amount of speculation. The first is an aperture in the lower end of the eastern stone, so

---

[1] Dr. Furgusson (*Rude Stone Monuments*, p. 100,) considers a trilithon, as an "improved dolmen."

much resembling an artificially constructed means of access to the chamber, that Norden does not hesitate to call it "the dore or Entrance."[1] The height of this "dore" is 2 feet, and its breadth 1 foot 9 inches. Mr. Pattison considers that it "exhibits marks of art;" but, on an examination of the stone in December, 1871, the author came to the conclusion that the fracture, if not the natural configuration of the stone, *might* have been accidentally caused either at the time of its transportation from the quarry, or during its erection. The second feature to be noticed is a hole, from six to eight inches in diameter, in the north-east corner of the covering stone. It is more oblong than round, and is placed immediately above the "entrance" just described. The circumstance of a hole being so frequently found in the dolmens of Eastern Europe and India, has induced some antiquaries to form a comparison between them and the Trethevy Stone; but in the former cases the hole is always in one of the side stones, and commu-

---

[1] A characteristic example of a dolmen with a rude door, formed by a piece having been cleft out of the lower part of one of the side stones, occurs at Grandmont, Bas-Languedoc, France. A drawing of this will be found in Dr. Furgusson's work, p. 344. Holed dolmens also are found in France, so that the idea in each case may be same.

A dolmen at Arroyolos, in Portugal, is also provided with a door; and instances might be quoted from Palestine and India.

In many cases, it must be remembered, dolmens have served as sheep-pens, and doors may have been cut to afford means of ingress or egress; though some of the foreign ones certainly do not admit of this solution of the difficulty.

nicates with the interior of the chamber, while in the latter it is pierced through an overlapping portion of the roof. Norden speaks of it as "an arteficiall holl, which served as it seemeth to putt out a staffe, whereof the house it selfe was not capable." Mr. Pattison confirms this opinion, by mentioning that "the sides are smooth as if worn by a staff;" and such is, without doubt, the true account of it. Another quotation from that gentleman's excellent paper, which, coming from a Fellow of the Geological Society, is of additional interest and value, may be added in conclusion. "The stones," he says, "composing this monument are all of granite, which occurs in boulders about half-a-mile distant. There is a broad upland valley intervening between Trethevy and the granite. The builders must therefore have credit for the exertion of combined strength and skill, in transporting these enormous masses of rock across the hollow, and up the hill on which they now stand."

ZENNOR CROMLECH.

Zennor Quoit, as the Cromlech in the parish of that name is usually called, was, when Borlase wrote his History, the most interesting and perfect specimen of a Kist-Vaen in Western Cornwall. In all probability it had been freshly disinterred from its cairn, or rather the gigantic structure had just succeeded in shaking off, or piercing up through, the crust of loose débris which had been piled over it; for in the middle of the last century, "a stone barrow, fourteen yards in diameter, was heaped round it, and almost reached to the edge of the Quoit."[1] Care had been taken, however, in its erection, that no stone should get into the chamber, and it was with great difficulty that a man could squeeze himself into it. Since then, progress and destruction, working together as usual, have much impaired the monument; the cap-stone has been rolled off, and the other stones otherwise damaged by being made to serve as the supports of a cart-shed. Fortunately an original drawing and a plan were made for Dr. Borlase's work, and these the author has been able to reproduce in woodcut from copies of the identical copper-plates then used. They will be found much more accurate and valuable than any sketch of the ruin, as it is at present, could possibly be.

The account which accompanies these engravings is as follows:—"On the top of a high hill about half-a-mile to the east of Senar Church-town stands a very large handsome Cromlêh; the area inclosed by the supporters is six feet eight inches by four feet, and points east and west. The Kist-Vaen is neatly formed, and fenced every way, and the (Eastern)

---

[1] The word "Quoit" is here used for the cap-stone only.

supporter is 8 feet 10 inches high, from the surface of the earth in the Kist-Vaen, to the under face of

ZENNOR CROMLECH. GROUND PLAN AND ELEVATION.
From Borlase's Antiquities.

the Quoit. The side stones of the Kist-Vaen, running on beyond the end stone, form a little cell to the east, by means of two stones terminating them at right angles. The great depth of this Kist-Vaen, which is about eight feet, at a medium under the plane of the Quoit, is remarkable. . . . . . . The Quoit was brought from a karn about a furlong off, which stands a little higher than the spot on which this Cromlêh is erected."[1]

The following measurements of the stones which compose this Cromlech were taken on the 17th of February, 1872, and very closely accord with those obtained by the scale which accompanies the plan at page 53.

		feet.		ft. in.		ft. in.
Covering Stone	Length..18,	breadth..	9 6,	thickness..	1 0
Stone on South side ..		height...	9 0,	breadth...	11 0
,, ,, West side ..		,,	4 0,	,,	3 0
,, ,, East side ...		,,	8 0,	,,	3 11
Two stones on North side (larger)		,,	7 0,	,,	7 0
(smaller)		,,	3 0,	,,	4 0
Two stones forming 2nd kist (N).		,,	6 10,	,,	10 6
(S).		,,	4 0,	,,	7 0

The apparent attempt made in this case to form a second Kist-Vaen is very remarkable. If it really be such, it is a unique instance in Cornwall of what is very commonly found in other Cromlech-bearing countries. It reminds us of those of Northern and Western Wales, and of Anglesea especially, where a small Kist-Vaen, side by side with the larger one, seems to be the rule and not the exception. In all instances, however, that the author has observed, that in the latter district, the smaller Cromlech has its own appropriate covering stone,[2] while at Zennor

---

[1] *Ant. of Cornwall*, p. 232, 2nd Edit. "Near this karn is another cromlêh" ('about 200 paces to the N.E. of the first' adds the MS.) "not so large as that here described; in other respects not materially different."—*Ibid.*

[2] Compare the ground plan of Zennor with that of Knockeen, county of Waterford. See *Rude Stone Monuments*, p. 230.

both were under one and the same roof. At Loch Maria Ker, in Brittany, and elsewhere in the same country, there seem to be examples much more in point. M. Fremenville observes in reference to one of them—"On s'apercoit que l'intérieur etait partagé en deux chambres par une cloison composée de deux pierres plantées sur champ. Ces séparations se remarquent dans beaucoup d'autres dolmens; plusieurs même sout divisés en trois chambres."[1] A drawing of the Cromlech at Loch Maria Ker will be found in Col. Forbes Leslie's Early Races of Scotland, Vol. ii., page 281.

It may be noticed that there are remains of ancient hut dwellings at Carne, about a furlong east of the Zennor Cromlech.

CHYWOONE CROMLECH.

The most perfect and compact Cromlech in Cornwall is now to be described. It is situated on the high ground that extends in a northerly and westerly direction from the remarkable megalithic fortification of Chywoone or Chuûn, in the parish of Morvah. The "Quoit" itself, which, seen from a distance, looks much like a mushroom, is distant just 260 paces from the gateway of the castle; and about the same distance on the other side of it, in the tene-

---

[1] Fremenville's *Antiquités de la Bretagne*, Morbihan, p. 23.

ment of Keigwin, is a barrow containing a deep oblong Kist-Vaen, long since rifled, and now buried in furze. Thinking this monument the most worthy of a careful investigation of all the Cromlechs in the neighbourhood, the author proceeded to explore it in the summer of 1871, with a view to determine, if possible, the method and means of erection in the case of such structures in general.

CHYWOONE CROMLECH.
From a Sketch by the Author.[1]

Sinking a pit by the side of the western stone, it was first of all discovered that the building rested on the solid ground, and not on the surrounding tumulus in which it had been subsequently buried. The Kist,

---

[1] There is a dolmen at Moytura, in Ireland, and another at Halskov, in Scandinavia, the drawings of which would both pass for Chywoone Cromlech.

as it seems, was formed in the following manner:—
The two upright stones forming the east and west
ends of the chamber were the first to be set up, at a
distance of about six feet apart; the breadth of the
latter is four feet, and of the former 3 feet 10 inches,
while the height of both is as nearly as possible
the same, 6 feet 4 inches. Another flat block of
granite, 8 feet 4 inches long, was then set up in a
slanting position against their northern edges, precisely as one places the third card in building a card
box, serving at the same time as a part of the fabric,
and as a stay or hold-fast to the sides against which
it rests. It was from this side, no doubt, and probably
over this slanting stone, that, with the assistance of
an embankment and rollers, the cap-stone was raised
into its present situation, from which, unlike Humpty
Dumpty, in the Nursery Rhyme, not all the adverse
combinations of subsequent ages have as yet been
able to displace it. This covering stone is a rough
slab of hard-grained granite, of a convex shape, and,
if the meaning of "vaulted" really enters into the
word Cromlech, it would be particularly applicable
in this instance. The length across the centre is
twelve feet, and the breadth the same, while in thickness it averages from fourteen inches to two feet.
The height of the interior of the Kist is seven feet;
and a small pit seems to have been sunk in the centre,
below the level of the natural soil. It is here that

the interment in all probability originally rested, and the chamber was then completed by a fifth stone (7 feet 8 inches long) thrown against the south side, but not reaching sufficiently high to come in contact with the covering stone. The barrow or cairn, which in some places nearly reaches the top of the side stones on the exterior, is thirty-two feet in diameter, and was hedged round by a ring of upright stones. In digging down some of this pile from the sides of the monument, it was discovered that the interstices between the side stones had been carefully protected by smaller ones, placed in such a manner as to make it impossible for any of the rubbish of the mound to find its way into the kist. This arrangement will be better understood by referring to the letters A A in the accompanying plan, and is

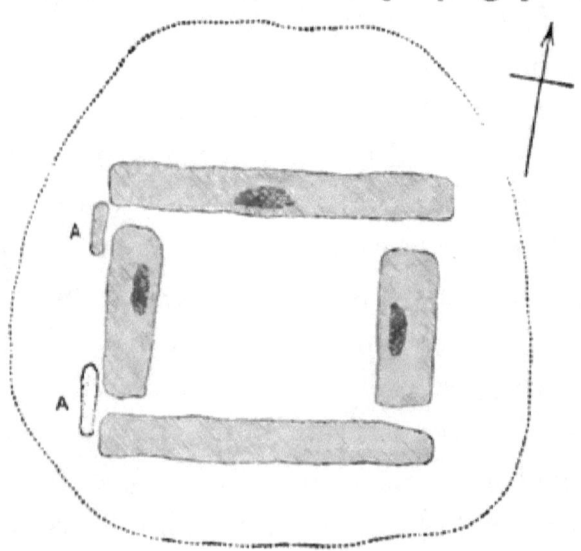

GROUND PLAN OF CHYWOONE.

very suggestive of the whole being once totally buried in the tumulus.

Among the heap of stones a small fractured piece of flint was discovered. Its shape, however, does not lead to the supposition that it was ever used as an instrument of any kind. A round cavity on the capstone seems to have been a work of modern times, and was probably the socket of a pole during the survey.

There are ruins of ancient hut-circles within the enclosure at Chuûn Castle, as also at Bossullo Crellas immediately below.

Of the Cornish Cromlechs which remain to be noticed, those at Mulfra and Bosporthennis, in the West, are dismantled; while that at Goss Moor, near St. Columb, is totally destroyed. The largest and more noteworthy of these is the Mulfra Quoit, situated on the summit of the hill of that name, some four miles north-west of Penzance.

MULFRA CROMLECH.

This monument consists at present of three granite slabs five feet in height, forming the west, north, and east sides of a kist 6 feet 8 inches long, *i.e.*, from east to west, and four feet wide from north to south. On the southern side, instead of the fourth slab, a stone, which is supposed to have been once the covering-stone, rests lengthways and obliquely against the edges of the side stones. This stone, the lower end of which is now fixed in the ground, measured, with "a piece evidently clove or broke off from it," in Borlase's time, 14 feet 3 inches long, by 9 feet 8 inches broad. At that time a stone-barrow, now entirely removed, measuring two feet high, and thirty-seven in diameter, surrounded the monument. There is little doubt that the removal of the southern supporter caused the overthrow of Mulfra Quoit. It might indeed be possible that the cap-stone was never actually raised to the position for which it was intended; but the fact of a fracture having taken place in it, as well as the angle at which it now stands, which is precisely that it would have assumed had it been overbalanced and slipped from its place, presents no analogy to the case of Lower Lanyon, and confirms the supposition that it is simply a fallen Cromlech. The author of the Land's End District states that, he was informed that the date of its collapse was 1752, during a thunderstorm. He was, however, probably misled by an account published in the Philosophical Transactions of the year following, in which it is recorded that a "quoit" on Mólfra Hill, (meaning the highest stone on a *natural* pile of rocks, and often so called by the Cornish), had been struck by lightning in that year. Dr. Borlase visited the spot on the 23rd of October,

1749, and at that time the Cromlech was in precisely the same state as at present. He says, "As this Quoit is off from its ancient situation with one edge resting on the ground, I thought it might permit us safely to search the enclosed area." Nothing of importance was discovered, and the Doctor only found that a pit had been sunk twenty inches deep in the area of the Kist-Vaen, and "that something which either was originally, or has since turned black, was placed in the bottom of it."

In the winter of 1871, the author caused a low cairn of stones, about thirty feet in diameter, and two feet high, on the northern brow of the hill on which this Cromlech stands, to be dug through. Pieces of charred wood, and a long smooth pebble, the size of a man's finger, was the only product of the exploration. Another barrow lay to the west of this one, but that also appeared to have been previously overhauled.

The ruins of hut circles are to be found on the southern slope of the hill.

QUOIT NEAR ST. COLUMB.

The hamlet of Quoit, in the parish of St. Columb Major, is situated at the foot of the gradual acclivity crowned by the circumvallations of Castle-an-dinas, and derives its name from a Cromlech, which, until a year or two since, occupied the corner of a yard adjoining the high road. On the side opposite to Castle-an-dinas stretches away the Goss Moor, "a morisch ground," as Leland well called it, "al baren of woodde." The monument was extant in a dismantled condition until very lately; but a few rough spar stones, split up and ready to carry away, was all that remained of it when the author saw the place in July, 1871. Previous to its fall, it had been used as a goat's house; and, oddly enough, although penned up within it at the time of the collapse, Billy escaped perfectly unharmed.

Old Hals mentions this Cromlech in his usual brief and inaccurate manner; but fortunately, Mr. Whitaker[1] has left a much more full and detailed account. From him we learn that it was "formed of five stones, one covering, three supporting, and one buttressing." The area of the chamber "allowed three or four men to stand upright within it." The side stone on the north was "a spar exactly perpendicular, seven feet in height, and 4 feet 6 inches in width at the middle." That opposite to it, on the south side, was "an iron-stone 6 feet 11 inches high, and 3 feet 7 inches wide in the middle." The eastern slab was also an iron-stone, "7 feet 6 inches in tallness, and 3 feet 3 inches wide at the middle." The covering-stone was of the same nature as the two

---

[1] *Cathedral of Cornwall*, vol. ii., p. 76.

last, and "lies reclining" from the eastern one along the two others, the declivity being "19 degrees 40 minutes from east to west." "I mention these little circumstances," continues Mr. Whitaker, "to explain clearly a peculiar incident in the construction of the whole; the northern corner of the back-stone appears to have broken off under the weight of the top-stone, as the latter was laid or was settling upon the former; and the top stone now touches not the back-stone in that corner at all, resting only on the other, the southern corner. In consequence of the accident, the whole weight nearly of the top-stone was *canted* off upon the adjoining side-stone on the right or south; *this* finding *that* to press with a force which it was not calculated to bear, began to shrink from its original uprightness, and to lean considerably towards the north; it would have leaned very considerably if the eastern edge of it had not lapped over the southern of the back stone, there impinged strongly upon this in its inclination, and been stopped by the resistance which it thus encountered: even with that resistance, it has come to lean no less than 16 degrees 30 minutes to the north, or two feet out of the true perpendicular. The whole building, therefore, was in the most imminent hazard of being soon off its poise, and the supporting stones were likely to be crushed to the ground by the covering stone. To prevent this, with the same skill and boldness which could raise such masses upon such supporters; which could also calculate the duration of a structure so warping; and even rest secure enough in their calculations to work under the warping structure, a fifth stone was introduced into it, being thrust in behind the side-stone on the north, as a buttress to the northern edge of the back-stone.[1] A stone was hastily chosen, tapering upwards in form, but about six feet in tallness, a kind of bastard spar, having two legs, a long and a short one, to it; the long leg was pitched in the ground, while the short remains above ground useless; and the body of the stone was then fixed reclining in a sharp angle against the edge of the back-stone, so as to compose a rude kind of powerful arc-boutant to it. Thus buttressed, the back-stone has remained between the supporting and the pressing stones, without any inclination at all to the north; yet, with a projection to the west, the quarter on which it felt no resistance, of 7 degrees 30 minutes, or one foot from the perpendicular. Thus has the structure stood as firm as if no misfortune had befallen it."

At the risk of some tediousness to the reader, this dry, though graphic description of the minutiæ of this monument, has been placed before him. In the absence of any drawing or ground plan, it affords

---

[1] Compare Trethevy.

all the details they could have furnished, and affords many points of comparison between this and other Cromlechs, both in Cornwall and elsewhere. In its original plan it seems not unlike the Kist-Vaen at Chywoone: the buttress is not an uncommon feature in Cromlechs generally, and has a counterpart in that of Trethevy, described at a previous page.

The several kinds of stone, used in the formation of this "Quoit," are common to the neighbourhood. The Pawton Cromlech, not many miles distant, is composed of a similar sparry stone. In all the other instances, however, granite has been the stone of the district, and therefore has been made use of; while the fact that at Trethevy it was brought from some little distance, seems to afford proof that it was the preferable material, where it was at all within reach.

Whether it be owing to a very extensive population in early times, or to the slow progress of the plough through its rocky and desolate crofts, the parish of Zennor on the northern coast of West Cornwall is a district still particularly fruitful in objects of interest to the Antiquary. One very large Cromlech in this parish has been already noticed, and the author of the "Land's End District" has recorded the existence of another, also "of considerable size," once standing on the estate of Trewey on the opposite hill. Mr. Edmonds also mentions a Kist-Vaen, "six or eight feet square," which, as a farmer informed him, occupied the bottom of a hollow in the centre of a barrow called Gundry Cave, one hundred feet in circumference, raised on the top of a natural "Karn" near the same place. This, like the former one, had been demolished.

BOSPORTHENNIS CROMLECH.

There still remains, however, a fourth Cromlech in Zennor parish, the ruins of which are to be found in a small enclosure near the hamlet of Bosporthennis. It is situated in a marshy valley, running down to the sea at Polmear Cove, skirted on the western side by the picturesque granite peaks of Carn Galva. On the slope of this hill, and some four or five hundred yards from the Cromlech, are the ruins of hut circles, strewn in such numbers over the moor, that it is clear they represent the ground plan of a town of considerable size. One of these huts is, perhaps, the best specimen of the beehive type to be found anywhere in England, and in the style of its masonry presents the same megalithic construction which distinguishes the works of the Cromlech-builders. On the cliffs at Bosigran, about half-a-mile distant, are the remains of one of those "cliff castles" so common on the Cornish coasts, and which, doubtless, served in dangerous times as refuges for the persons and effects of the inhabitants of the surrounding villages.

Bosporthennis Cromlech stands at present in the centre of a small mound of stones and earth, which once, no doubt, covered the whole structure. Many smaller mounds occur in the same enclosure, but in one of them, lately explored, nothing remarkable was found; though a farmer asserted that many "cloam"[1] pots, and ashes had been taken from barrows on an adjacent hill. The Kist-Vaen in this case is smaller than any of those already noticed, being only five feet in length by three in breadth; and therefore could scarcely have received a body at full length. The height of the side stones is between four and five feet; two of them stand in their original position; one is thrown down, and the fourth has been removed. But the principal feature in this Cromlech, when it was discovered a few years since, was, that it had a *circular covering-stone*, six inches thick, and five feet in diameter, lying in the area described by the supporters. This was at once pronounced to be unique.

---

[1] "Cloam," a word used by the common people for earthenware. A "cloam buzza," is "an earthenware milk pan" in Cornwall. An eminent philologist, when asked the derivation of the word, at once replied "clay loam."

The fame of the discovery quickly spread. The Local Antiquarianism of the whole neighbourhood was awakened immediately, and savans of all shapes, sexes, and ages, "visited and inspected" the stone. The sphere for conjecture was of course unlimited, and ranged from Arthur's round table, to the circular tombs of modern Bengal. Two things were clear at all events : there were stone-cutters among the Cromlech-builders; and the excellent idea of a circle proved the knowledge of the compass! But, alas! the mantle of Edie Ochiltree had fallen this time on a Celt of another family, on a genuine Cornu-Briton! Edging his way through the crowd which surrounded the monument, until he had reached the front rank, an old man was heard dispelling the fond illusion in the following cruel words : " Now what are 'e all tellin' of? I do mind when uncle Jan, he that was miller down to Polmeor, cum' up 'long to the croft a speering round for a fitty stoan of es mill. And when he had worked 'pon that theere stoan ; says he : I'll be jist gone to knack un a bit round like ; so he pitched to work ; but e would'nt sarve es purpose, so theere 'e es still. And, lor bless yer all, a fine passel o' pepple has been heere for to look 'pon un, but what they sees en un es more than I can tell 'e."

This was "minding the bigging o't" with a vengeance, and the antiquaries could only console themselves in the reflection that the stone must have been of a rudely circular form to have induced the miller to try his tool upon it at all.

When the author saw it in December, 1871, some of the splintered pieces were lying round, and he is led to imagine that the original shape was oblong.

Since the above description of Bosporthennis Cromlech was written, the author accompanied the Rev. W. S. Symonds, F.G.S., to the spot, and caused the floor of the structure to be carefully cleared out. Resting on the natural soil, was found a deposit of burnt bones, some of them adhering to the fragments of a globular vessel. The pottery was of a greenish black colour, not unlike the Upchurch ware, and was half the thickness of the average sepulchral pottery found in Cornwall. A fractured flint, and two stones of the nature of Jasper were found with the bones. These are now in the Museum of Sir W. Jardine, Bart.

CHAMBERED TUMULI.

Professor Nillson has divided the sepulchres of Sweden into the dösar or Cromlechs, and the ganggrifter, passage or gallery graves. As the list of the former is now, as far as Cornwall is concerned, completed, the question arises, "are there any of the latter class"? In the precise sense which the term "passage grave" conveys to a Swedish antiquary, there certainly are not; that is, there is not one single instance of the *long* side gallery. But, in the general sense of the word, there are several instances of passage tombs, that is, long chambers buried in tumuli, and roofed in with large flat stones, and in two cases at least provided with a short and narrow means of egress to the side of the mound. Chambered tumuli are common to all parts of the world, from the famous

New Grange, in Ireland, or Maeshow, in Orkney, to the almost similar structures of Asia Minor, and the East. Sometimes they take the form of a contiguous line of Cromlechs like the Grotto d' Else in France; sometimes their sides are constructed of layers of stone fitted together with more or less pretension to masonic skill.

The examples from Scilly and the mainland of Cornwall, which are now to be noticed, may be most fitly compared with others in the British Isles, (especially with one specimen from Dunmore, in Ireland, figured in the Kilkenny Archæological Society's publication for 1868); but it is a fact worthy of remark, that in Cornwall as in Denmark, these chambers are known by the name of "Giants' Graves." Only two groups of them occur; one being on the Island of St. Mary's, Scilly, and the other equally near the sea in the parish of Zennor on the mainland. Indeed, their proximity to the sea may render it not improbable, that wherever they are found, both here and elsewhere in the British Isles, they are the work of foreign mariners, perhaps of the marauding Danes themselves; or, if this may be considered as too modern an origin for them, of a no less piratical race coming, it may be, from the same country and infesting the same coasts as their historical successors.

Of the Scillonian examples Borlase gives the

following account :[1] "The ancient Sepulchres of
"this Island (St. Mary's) are either Caves, or, as
"they are called by some authors, Barrows. Of
"Caves, the Giant's Cave, near Tol's Hill, is the
"most remarkable ; the description of this may give
"you a just notion of the rest, but that they are
"neither so large nor so entire. The mouth of it is
"four feet six inches wide, it is thirteen feet eight
"inches long, and three feet eight high; we that were
"living were forced to creep into it, but it may admit
"*Giants* when they are dead. It is covered from
"end to end with large flat stones, which shelter the
"sheep, and has a tumulus of rubbish on the top
"of all.

"The Barrows here and in the adjacent Island
"are very numerous, and constructed in one manner.
"The outer ring is composed of large stones pitch'd
"on end, and the heap within consists of smaller
"stones, clay, and earth mix'd together ; they have
"generally a cavity of stone work in the middle
"covered with flat stones, but the Barrows are of
"various dimensions, and the cavities, which, being
"low and covered with rubble, are scarce apparent
"in some, consist of such large materials in others,

---

[1] Observations on the Ancient and Present State of the Islands of Scilly, in a letter to Charles Lyttelton, LL.D., by William Borlase. Oxford, 1756, p. 28.

"that they make the principal figure in the whole
"monument.

"We pitched upon a hill where there are many
"of these Barrows, and, as the common story goes,
"Giants were buried, with a design to search them,
"and on Wednesday, June the third, having hired
"some soldiers, proceeded to open them.

Fig. 1.

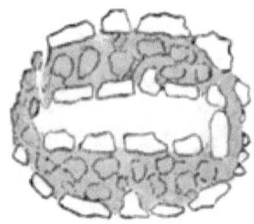

Fig. 2.

GIANTS' GRAVES AT SCILLY.
From Drawings by Dr. Borlase.

"In the first (fig. 1) we found no bones, nor urns,
"but some strong unctuous earth, which smelt cada-
"verous. In the middle of this Barrow was a large
"cavity full of earth :[1] there was a passage[2] into it
"at the eastern end one foot eight inches wide betwixt
"two stones set on end; the cavity was four feet eight

---

[1] The Giants' Chambers of Denmark (Jœttestuer) were filled with earth. See Worsaae, translated by Thoms, p. 87.

[2] In imitation perhaps of the side passages in the graves of Sweden.

"inches wide in the middle, the length of it twenty-
"two feet; it was walled on each side with masonry
"and mortar, the walls or sides four feet ten inches
"high; at the western end it had a large flat stone
"on its edge which terminated the cavity; it's length
"bore east by north, and it was covered from end to
"end with large flat stones, several of which we re-
"moved, and others had been carried off before for
"building the new Pier.

"Forty-two feet distant to the north, we opened
"another Barrow (fig. 2.) of the same kind; the cave
"was less in all respects, the length fourteen feet,
"bearing north-east by east, the walled sides two feet
"high; where narrowest, one foot eight inches; in the
"middle, four feet wide; in the floor was a small
"round cell dug deeper than the rest. In this we
"found some earths of different colours from the
"natural one, but nothing decisive. It was covered
"with flat stones like the former."

The second group of chambered tumuli is situated near the village of Treen or Treryn, in the parish of Zennor. These are three in number, the third lying about half-a-mile to the east of the other two, close to the hamlet of Pennance. Of these barrows, the latter is the largest, and also the most perfect; one of the others nearly equals it in size, but the third is much smaller. An excellent description of the Pennance chamber, accompanied by woodcuts from the pencil of Mr. J. T. Blight, will be found in the *Gentleman's Magazine* for July, 1865.

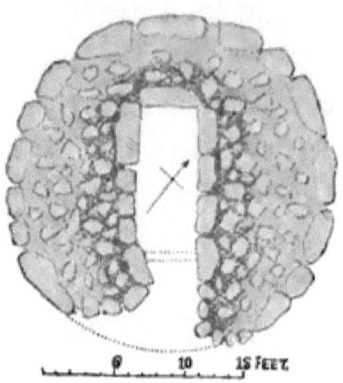

PLAN OF PENNANCE BARROW.
From a Drawing in the Gentleman's Magazine.

That gentleman very justly describes the structure as "an intermediate step between the simple rectangular Kist-Vaen of a Cromlech, and the subterranean galleries," or underground habitations common to Cornwall, as well as other Celtic countries. The chamber at Pennance measures 9 feet 6 long, by four feet wide, and is 4 feet 4 high. As in the Scilly Barrows, the roof is formed of large slabs of granite, and Mr. Blight has noticed that the "first slab of the roof is lower than the others, the height from the floor to its under surface being 3 feet 6 inches only," and that "it has the appearance of being designed as a lintel" for the entrance, which was therefore probably at that end.

The walls of the chamber are formed of neat

masonry, similar to the hedging work still in use in the neighbourhood. It is covered by a tumulus seventy feet in circumference, built round at its base with large stones, and measuring eight feet in height. The chamber lies N.W. by S.E.

One solitary example of a chambered tumulus has still to be noticed. It is situated in a field near the village of Chapel Euny, in the parish of Sancreed, and was first discovered by the author in the month of April, 1863, at the time when he was exploring a subterranean structure about a quarter of a mile distant.[1]

BARROW NEAR CHAPEL EUNY. FRONT VIEW.
From a Sketch by the Author.

The peculiarity of this tumulus is, that it combines within itself the features of the stone grave, the ring-barrow, the cromlech, and the passage chamber, and

---

[1] See Proceedings of the Society of Antiquaries of London, Nov., 1868.

it seems indeed to supply a connecting link between them all in the chain of the megalithic series. The valley in which it stands is surrounded on all sides by ancient remains. Tredinney, where part of a gold bracelet of the ring-money type was found, and also where a barrow containing an urn has been explored,[1] lies to the west. More to the north are the circles of Bartinney, mentioned in Borlase's Cornwall; between these and Brane Castle lie the Chapel Euny huts and cave; while to the east the "Castellum Brenni," or Caer Bran, crowns the summit of a rising ground.

It will be observed by referring to the plan p. 77, that the sepulchral chamber is concealed like that at Pennance in a tumulus of a conical form, the base being encircled and supported by large granite stones set on edge, the highest of which is four feet above the ground. The height of the tumulus is eight feet, and the circumference fifty. The internal dimensions of the chamber are as follows:—Length, six feet. Breadth, from three feet at the entrance, which is fronting the south, to 3 feet 9 inches at the northern and opposite end. Height, 3 feet 6 inches. The sides and end of the chamber are formed of single blocks of granite, resting, not on the natural soil, but on a small artificial elevation of about two

---

[1] See the account of this at a subsequent page.

feet in height. They are covered in by *two* roofing stones, respectively measuring 5 feet 6, by 3 feet 6, and 2 feet 5. A stone at the end of the eastern slab, which is not so high as the others, seems to point to a similar construction in this case to that at Pennance, namely, a depressed entrance to the central chamber.

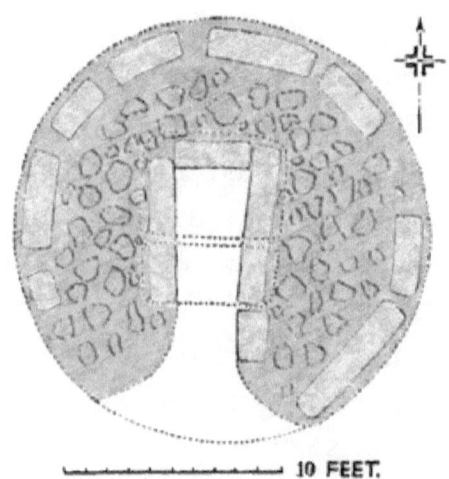

GROUND PLAN OF CHAPEL EUNY BARROW.
From a Drawing by Mrs. W. C. Borlase.

When this barrow was opened no one knows, and the farmer assured the author that the only reason he had not carried it away was, that it afforded a convenient shelter for sheep or pigs. It may fairly be considered as the most perfect of its kind in the West of England.

The extreme rarity of authentic instances of *extended* inhumation in Cornwall will have been fully realised during the perusal of the preceding pages.

The evidence of *contracted* interments, though more authentic is equally meager. In many of the Kist-Vaen Cromlechs, indeed, it is more probable that the latter practice was adopted than the former; but where there is positively nothing to show for either opinion, speculation is worse than useless. Evidence has just been adduced which shows that one at least of the larger Kists contained a burnt interment, (see p.   note) and whether there was any reason to suppose that the contracted method, so common, and proved to be so primitive, in the North of England, ever found its way to Cornwall at all, might, until a recent discovery presently to be narrated, have been a point very fairly disputed. Stone graves have, indeed, been found, sometimes occupying the centre of a stone cairn, sometimes stumbled into by the tourist in his rambles over the heath, which are certainly much too contracted ever to have received a body at full length. True it is that, as will be seen at a future page, urns and ashes have been found in some of these, but there are also instances where the author has searched in vain, both in and around them, for any trace of incineration, or even burnt earth or stones. On the downs lying between the Morvah hill barrow, and the Men-an-tol, or famous holed stone, were a large number of these graves, until their granite sides and covers were, a few years since, carried away to make some waterfalls in the gardens at

Castle Horneck. Dr. Borlase has preserved an account of the accidental discovery of a Kist of this description, in which large human bones were found.[1] As these appear not to have been burnt, there may be an instance here, though a very doubtful one, of the actual disinterment of a contracted body, buried in its entirety. The account is as follows :—[2]

"About the year 1716, Matthew Williams, of Maen (near the Land's End), wanting some stones for building, and passing along the lane which leads from Maen to Sennen Church, about midway betwixt the church and the village, the mason with him struck his iron barr on a flatt stone, 6 foot by 7, and finding it to sound hollow, advised Williams to take up that stone as very proper for his service. The stone came up easily, and to their great surprise a square cavity appeared, at the end of which was a stone about two feet long, and a stone about four foot long on each side. In the middle of this cavity was a clay pott or urne full of earth as black as soot,

---

[1] Mr. J. G. Fuller, of Camelford, has recently most kindly supplied the author with the account of what appears to be an undoubted example of contracted interment discovered in a barrow at Lesnewth, near Tintagel.

A cell, nine inches deep, was found under a pile of stones in the centre of the tumulus, covered by a slab 4 feet 3 long, by 3 feet 3 broad. This contained a skeleton, which must of necessity have been disjointed or contracted, as the bones were proved to be those of an unusually tall man. A legend, told by the crones of the neighbourhood, recorded that a gigantic figure could often be seen on the top of this mound.

[2] Parochial Memoranda, MS. p. 23.

and round the urne very large human bones scattered irregularly and not placed in their natural order; several bitts of brass were found, supposed to be part of an helmet buried with the bones, and Williams shewed us the point of a brazen sword found at the same time and place, the piece had the thickness in the middle, and declined thinner towards the edges, as swords generally have, and the reason why the point should endure the violence of time and moisture more than any other part of the sword was likely owing to its being better tempered and hardened than the rest as more used to execution. It was incrusted with the green rust of copper, so that any one might take it for pure copper as the owner did, till on his cutting it at our desire it appeared to be true brass. July 12th, 1742."

But however doubtful an instance this may be, of the practice in Cornwall of contracting the corpse, the following details will be sufficient to shew that there is in the west at least one genuine example of the mode of burial so general in the North of England.

THE TREVELGUE, OR TREVALGA TUMULI.

About a quarter of a mile east of the curious, and partly insulated, entrenchments known as Trevelgue Cliff Castle, there are situated, on the property of Lord Churston, two exceedingly fine barrows. They occupy not only the highest position on the cliff, but the summit of one of the most commanding elevations in the district, whence they are clearly distinguishable for many miles round.

On the 7th of March, 1872, a party of gentlemen, among whom were Mr. Spence Bate, F.R.S.; Captain Oliver; Mr. Evans; the Revd. W. Iago, and Mr. R. N. Worth, very kindly accompanied the author, to take advantage of the permission granted him to explore the mounds. The distance between the two is thirty-eight paces, and their northern bases are connected by a low semicircular bank of earth. They point in a direction E.N.E. and W.S.W. The westernmost of the two measures 250 feet in circumference; the greatest axis being from E. to W., in which direction the diameter is 100 feet. Eleven feet represents the height of this mound in the centre.

Driven by the weather to the northern and sheltered side, the workmen began by cutting a trench towards the middle. At a depth of two or three feet from the surface, it became evident that the entire substratum consisted of burnt earth, quite as red and almost as fine as brick dust; of this there were several hundred cartloads.[1] Observing that the

---

[1] A paper on the subject of these tumuli was read to the Society of Antiquaries on the 2nd of May, 1872. The quantity of burnt earth is most re-

colour became more intense on the eastern side, it was determined to follow it in that direction, and before long a pile of stones, many of them brought from the beach, and much blackened by fire, was found to be lying beneath the red earth. This heap was about twelve feet in diameter, and four feet high. On reaching the opposite side of it, the burnt earth was found to be worked out. Under the "cairn," however, lay a large spar, singularly flat for a stone of that nature, which, by the bye, does not occur *in situ*. It measured 10 feet 6 inches long, 5 feet 6 inches broad, and 1 foot 9 inches thick. The outer edge was only twenty-four feet from the eastern side of the tumulus, and from that direction a pit was accordingly sunk beside it. The stone was then seen to be lying on a level with the surrounding soil of the country. A pit had, however, been sunk under it, into the sides of which, four slate stones set on their edges, and averaging seven or eight inches thick, had been inserted. These formed the sides of a chamber of which the large spar stone was the covering.[1] Being anxious to ascertain the contents of the tomb, and not liking to remove

---

markable, both when the reduction caused by the fire from the original quantity, and when the time that must have elapsed during the process of incineration is taken into account.

[1] Were it not sunk beneath the soil, this chamber might, from its proportions, be justly called a Dolmen, or Cromlech of the Kist-Vaen class.

either of the side-stones, (upon all four of which the cap-stone rested), the author caused a piece of one of the slates, already fractured, to be removed. An entrance for the body being thus effected, the internal dimensions of the chamber were measured as follows:—Length, 6 feet 2 inches; breadth, 2 feet 6 inches; height, 2 feet 9 inches. So well were the slabs fitted together that no earth had found its way in. The floor seemed originally to have been paved with slates, but many of these had been by some means or other displaced, and, strange to say, portions of a skull were taken up from below instead of above them.

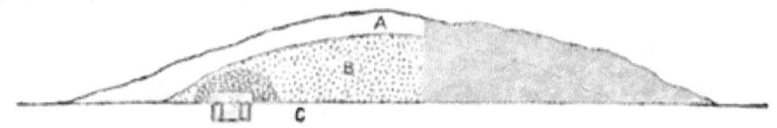

SECTION OF THE WESTERN BARROW, TREVELGUE.
From a Drawing by the Author.

Along the centre of the grave, which lay N.W. and S.E., was strewn a quantity of brownish mould interspersed with particles of white matter, evidently decayed bone. The skull lay close against the N.W. end; small portions of it were alone preserved, but these were of an unusual thickness. The bones were unburnt, but in what position the body had been placed it was impossible to determine; although the subsequent discovery of a contracted interment in a similar chamber makes it most probable that such was also the position in this instance.

From the fact of unburnt remains being found beneath the burnt stones and earth above mentioned, it would seem that a fire had been lighted on the roof of the grave subsequently to the burial; and so great was the quantity of burnt matter, that it is probable that these fires were alight, and the funeral feasts kept up for several weeks, perhaps months together.

Amongst the stones which composed the pile was a slate, about one foot in diameter, perforated, and slightly concave, very similar to the granite mills, found near British huts. A small piece of thin Roman, or late Celtic, pottery of the domestic type was found in the débris of the mound, as also several small pebbles and a rough flint chip.

The second and eastern barrow was opened on Monday, March 11th, 1872. This measured eighty-six feet in diameter, and was thirteen feet high. From the greater acclivity of its sides, it is far the most conspicuous object of the two, and the shape is rather that of the "bell" than the "bowl" barrow; at the summit was a depression of some eighteen inches. The workmen proceeded to sink a shaft twelve feet in diameter from the top to the centre. Immediately under the turf they found a bed of stones to the depth of three feet (A); under this, a stratum of hard clay, brought from a neighbouring valley, to the depth of five feet (B); under this again a second layer of stone, like the first, three feet deep; and lastly, under all, an immense slate stone, traversed with spar, and evidently transported thither from the cove below.

There was no red earth as in the other mound, but at the depth of five feet from the surface, among the clay, a secondary interment, consisting of a deposit of burnt bones and ashes, was discovered. These were protected by no covering stone, and were observed to be immediately over the centre of the large flat stone beneath. They were about a quart in all, and among them was a single flint chip.[1]

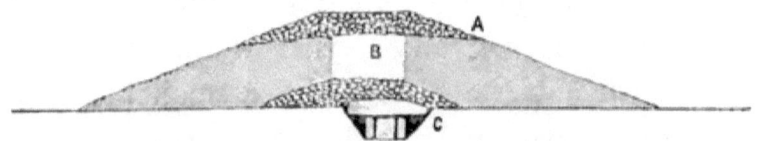

SECTION OF EASTERN BARROW, TREVELGUE.

On arriving at the flat stone it was found, like the other, to be on a level with the natural soil (C), and, like that one also, to be the covering of a sepulchral chamber. A pit was accordingly sunk at one end of it, and an entrance effected, not without some difficulty, owing to the fact that the covering stone in this instance overlapped the side-stones by several

---

[1] The abundance of flints in this neighbourhood is noticed at a subsequent page.

feet. As in the former case, the vault lay N.W. and S.E. In length it measured 5 feet 2 inches; in breadth 2 feet 10 inches, and in height (including a pavement six inches deep) 2 feet 9 inches. Owing to the depth of the mound, the covering stone could not be entirely laid bare. Its dimensions, however, cannot have been less than nine feet by ten, with a thickness averaging two feet; it therefore weighed many tons.

On the pavement of the vault lay a skeleton on its left side;[1] the head being at the N.E. corner, nearly a foot from the end wall. The legs were bent at the knees, and the arms stretched out, so that the hands must have touched the knees, or nearly so. The body had thus been contracted into a space not more than four feet long. Just at the spot where the hands would have been, lay a small perforated axe-hammer, beautifully fashioned out of a granitic stone, containing felspar, quartz, and shorl,[2] and measuring four inches in length.[3] This curious little relic was taken out perfect, but the bones on being touched, instantly crumbled away. One of the

---

[1] This is the usual position of the contracted interments in other parts of England. See *Bateman's Ten Years' Diggings*, &c., &c.

[2] The fact that this stone is found *in situ*, is suggestive of the native origin of the deceased.

[3] A very similar little axe-head is preserved at Penrose. It was found with several others in a field at Venton Vedna, whence it was brought to J. J. Rogers, Esq.

lumbar vertebræ, however, measured two inches in transverse diameter, by 1/10 inch in thickness. Axe-heads, similar to the one here described, have rarely been found in England;[1] and in France they are still more uncommon: in Ireland and Scotland, they are more plentiful, and in Germany they are common.[2]

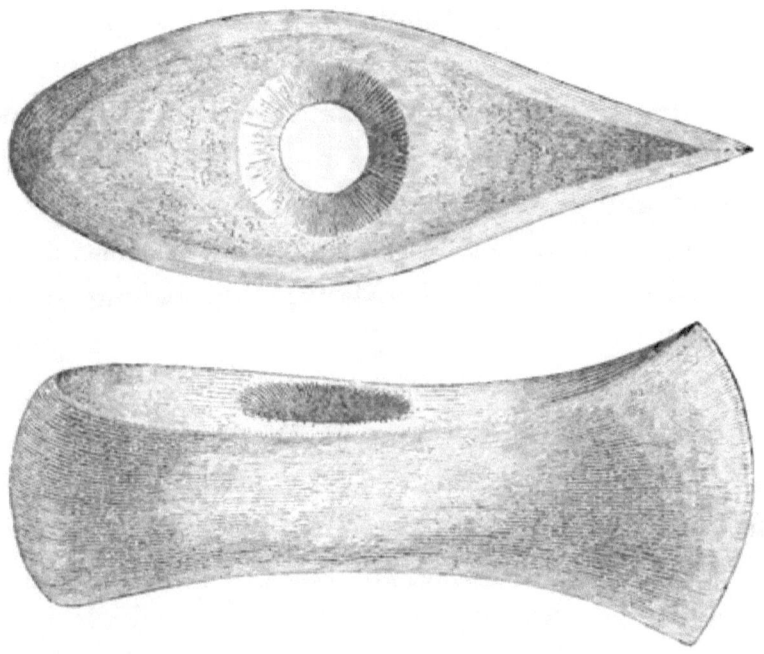

STONE AXE-HAMMER. TREVELGUE.

In several instances they have accompanied bronze

---

[1] Bateman gives a parallel example to this Trevelgue one. See "Ten Years' Diggings," p. 24. See also Nilsson, *Stone Age*, p. 60, edit. by Sir J. Lubbock.

[2] *Horæ Ferales*, p. 139, Pl. iii.

daggers of an antique type. In Scotland they are known by the name of Purgatory hammers.[1] "Found, as they frequently were," says Dr. Wilson, "within the cist, and beside the mouldering bones of their old Pagan possessors, the simple discoverer could devise no likelier use for them than that they were laid there for their owners to bear with them 'up the trinal steps,' and with them to thunder at the gates of purgatory." The more probable solution of the difficulty, as regards the smaller ones at least, is, that they were ornamental[2] rather than useful; but whether any peculiar ceremony or superstition caused them to be laid beside the dead, it is impossible to say. Sir John Lubbock believes they belong to the 'Bronze Age.' (*Prehist. Times*, New Edit., p. 91).

From the details here given of the exploration of these two graves, it must be at once admitted that they belong to a class of interment, as primitive in character, as they are rare in the district where they occur ; and in concluding the account of them, it may be observed that the connecting link, which their contents have supplied between the ancient inhabitants of Danmonia, and their North country contemporaries, is exceedingly valuable and instructive

---

[1] *Prehist. Annals.* Vol. i., p. 192.
[2] The author has been informed that in some savage communities stone celts are carried by the principal men, just as light canes are carried in England.

to the Prehistoric Archæologist. Indeed, there cannot be a shadow of doubt that, *if of native origin*, they belong to an earlier date than can be fairly assigned to any other interment mentioned in this volume. It is not, however, impossible that they are *not* of native origin, but are the traces of an intruding people, a party perhaps of the earliest Norsemen, whose galleys sailed forth in quest of adventure in the sunny southern clime. This idea is strengthened by two considerations. Firstly, the position of the barrows on the edge of the cliff, which will remind the reader at once of the grave of Beowulf, raised high on Hroness in order that his kindred rovers might behold it, as

> "Their beak-carved gallies,
> Out of hazy distance,
> Float haughtily by."

And secondly, the fact that while such interments are almost unique in Cornwall, they are well known to be common both to the Northern parts of Great Britain, and to the whole of Scandinavia.[1]

Whatever these speculations may be worth, the discovery of a contracted interment, in a megalithic grave, in company with a stone hammer, in Corn-

---

[1] For evidences of this the reader is referred to Mr. Bateman's *Ten Years' Diggings*; to those researches which Canon Greenwell has already made public, and to the excellent little volume of Worsaae, edited by Thoms.

wall, is an Archæological fact well worthy of record.

The division of the subject of this essay into two distinct classes of interments, inhumation and cremation, now brings the reader to the second of the two.

Whether, in point of time, the former or the latter custom claims priority in the annals of the human race is a question for those to decide who have made the origin of civilization their special study. Speaking, however, on the general merits of the question, there certainly seems a degree of refinement in the ceremony of incremation, which would scarcely have suggested itself to man in his primitive state; but, on the other hand, the necessity for such a course must have almost immediately forced itself upon the denizens of a sultry or tropical climate, where to bury the bodies in shallow graves unburnt would only be to spread pestilence far and near.

That the custom of cremation originated in a tropical clime is indeed almost beyond a doubt. In South America[1] the funeral pile is quite as fully recognised as a national institution among native tribes, as ever it is in India. Britain has therefore

---

[1] Dr. Daniel Wilson, *Prehistoric Man*, Vol. ii, p. 291, makes the following curious remark :—" Mummification, cremation, urn-burial, and inhumation were all in use among different tribes and nations of South America, and have left their traces no less unmistakeably on the northern continent."

received it from the south, but whether brought northward and westward by an intruding race, or copied from the custom of other countries, at a period not earlier than the contact with Roman civilization, it is hard to say. To the latter belief, as will appear in the sequel, the author is more disposed to lean.

When the question is asked generally, "Have there been found in the British Isles any interments, which can with some certainty be said to have preceded the practice of cremation," the answer must be that there are; but when a similar question is put with regard to Cornwall in particular, the answer is much more doubtful.

In the North of England the great proportion of primary interments in tumuli have been found to be unburnt bodies; while incinerated remains have been accumulated subsequently round the edges of the mound. But, after all, what does this prove? Not surely that cremation was universally introduced into these islands as a usage absolutely unknown to the builders of the mounds, at any definite period after their construction, or by any distinct race of conquerors; not, in short, that its appearance marked the commencement of an epoch in our primitive history; but simply that at the time when the urns and ashes were deposited, that mode of burial had come more into fashion in that particular neighbourhood, among people who recognised the mounds as the burial places of their family or their friends.

But even allowing that these contracted interments of the north and east of England belong to a date when cremation was absolutely unknown, the case is otherwise in Cornwall. The instances of contracted interments are so rare, and (with the exception of that at Trevelgue), so ill-authenticated, that nothing can be judged from them; while several of the long graves seem even to point to Christian times and observances. On the other hand, however, some of the instances of cremation, which will be found in the following pages, are so extremely rude, that none other than a most primitive people could (it will be said), have interred their dead in such a manner.

Taking these facts into consideration, the only position which, with regard to Britain generally, it really seems safe to adopt is, that among the earliest inhabitants of whose sepulchral rites there is any distinct trace, the two modes of disposing of the dead (viz., cremation and inhumation) existed side by side, but that cremation finally gained the ascendancy which it had always held in some districts, and which it continued to hold down to Christian times. Thus, in the Sepulchral Chamber at l'Ancresse, in Guernsey, Mr. Lukis found examples of contracted inhumation in close proximity to calcined bones, and urns. And, not to go out of England or even Cornwall for an instance, the larger Kist-Vaen at Lower Lanyon contained an entire carcass in company with an urn. Even if the over-strained theory of primary and secondary interments be brought into requisition to account for this, it can hardly be taken as evidence of the intrusion in the meantime of a different race of men.

It is hoped that the difficulties which, owing to the present empty state of the monuments, have beset the earlier parts of this enquiry, will be less felt in the pages which follow. Fire is a great preservative, so much so, indeed, that in some localities it is customary to bury charred wood under the boundary stones of landed property, in order that should any dispute subsequently arise, the presence or absence of this durable matter under the stone might at once settle the question. But the gain which, in this respect, the Antiquary may experience in the preservation of the bones or relics is unfortunately more than counterbalanced by the destruction of the skulls, as by this means he is deprived of the most valuable criterion, though, perhaps also the most perplexing object of study, which has occurred to modern ethnology.

To proceed, then, to the rudest and most primitive examples which Cornwall affords of the practice of cremation.

THE MENHIRION.

No pre-historic monument is so common in Cornwall as the Menhir, or as it is now called the "Long Stone." The researches made by the author at the foot of more than one of these rude pillars, lead him to conclude, with Sir John Lubbock, that, like the Gallan or Leagann, of Ireland, the Maen-gwyr, of Wales, and the Hare Stone, of Scotland, they were "sometimes tombstones, sometimes memorials of important events," and that the period of their erection ranges from very early far down into historic times. Some, slightly more symmetrical than the others, are graced with a simple inscription in plain bold Roman characters, recording the name of an individual, coupled by "filius" with that of his parent, and perhaps a military title. Others, extremely rude and of considerable height and bulk, are simply pitched on end in a shallow cavity sunk in the natural soil, typical in themselves of the rude ages in which they were set up, and of the almost superhuman force used by those who were engaged in the task. That this class of monument was much more frequent in Cornwall than at present is evident from the recurrence in the Tithe Apportionments of such names as "Long Stone Croft," "Field," "Downs," &c., indicating localities where no such remains now exist. The more ancient Celtic equivalent is found in the words Men or Maen, Menheniot, Hangman (Hen Maen), Menheer, and Tremenheere. Speaking of the last instance, Dr. Borlase mentions in his MSS. having seen an upright stone of this description standing on the farm of that name, in the parish of Ludgvan; and it is curious to notice that the ancient Cornish family, who own the name and estate of Tremenheere, bear for their arms,— Sable, three Doric columns, pale-wise, Argent; thus showing that when this "canting" coat was assumed, the meaning of the Celtic word was fully comprehended.

Of the monuments of this kind which still remain, the greater part owe their preservation to the use they are put to, as rubbing stones for cattle. Veneration for them, if it ever existed, has quite died out, or is only retained in some such Post-Reformation absurdity, as that they are persons turned into stone for neglecting the rigid observance of the Sabbath. In some countries, as their original meaning was forgotten, superstition afforded them an idolatrous sanctity, and at one in especial at Kerloaz, in Brittany, (forty feet high), Venus is said to be worshipped by "Pagan" votaries of the present day. At Loch Maria Ker in the same country, a spot famous for its cromlech and other megalithic remains, a monolith, now prostrate and broken, is said, when erect, to have attained the monstrous altitude of sixty feet. That at Rudston, in Yorkshire, is twenty-six feet above the ground, and twelve below. Worsaae says that the "Bautastene," "memorial stones" of Norway range from nine to twenty feet in height; an average which would correspond very closely to that of the Cornish ones, and indeed of those in the British Isles in general. Dr. Borlase gives[1] the following account of one at Men-Pern,[2] (in Cornish the "stone of sorrow)," in the parish of Constantine. "About four years since, in the garden adjoining to the house, stood a very tall stone, twenty feet above the ground, and four feet below; it was pyramidal in shape, and made above twenty stone posts for gates clove up by ye farmer, who gave me the account, September 29th, 1752."

Two monoliths, called the Pipers, at Boleit, in Buryan, measure respectively fifteen feet, and 13 feet 6 inches above ground.

In the neighbourhood of St. Columb many of these pillar stones may still be seen. Two of the most remarkable are situated on the St. Breock downs, the tallest (13 feet 6 inches in height) on the summit of the beacon hill, and the shorter (eight feet high) on a less elevated slope, some eight or nine hundred

---

[1] *Parochial Memoranda.* MS., p. 58.
[2] Perhen is "a purchaser," from perna "to buy;" but Pern is also "Sorrow." Hence, this stone may have been either the "witness" of a contract, or a burial place. Often, however, where etymologists puzzle themselves over a word of this kind, the most probable solution of the difficulty is that it is after all nothing more than a proper name.

yards to the east. Both these stones are spar stones, common to the country, rudely pitched on end in the ground, the largest of the two inclining considerably

MONOLITHS ON ST. BREOCK DOWNS.
From a Sketch by the Author.

to the north. About 150 yards S.W. of the taller stone and upon equally high ground lies a flat stone, also a spar, 9 feet 6 inches long, by six feet broad at its greatest breadth, resting on the ground at its northern edge, and at its southern, diagonally upon a second stone, 7 feet 6 inches long, by 2 feet 6 inches in breadth, and about the same in height above the ground. It has all the appearance of an imperfectly formed Kist-Vaen,[1] and therefore should perhaps have been inserted at a previous page.

A barrow of small stones, from thirty to forty feet in diameter, lies round it, and a farmer mentioned

---

[1] This species of monument is sometimes called an "earth-fast Cromlech;" sometimes a "demi-dolmen". Examples are not uncommon in Brittany, and one at Kerland (*Rude Stone Monuments*, p. 346) bears a strong resemblance to the above.

the fact that an old man in digging among them had once discovered *something* curious, but of what nature he could not remember. A small cairn also sur-

KIST-VAEN, OR "EARTH-FAST" CROMLECH, ST. BREOCK BEACON.
From a Sketch by the Author.

rounded the adjacent monolith, while barrows are scattered in abundance over the neighbouring downs.

Some idea of the St. Breock Monoliths may be formed from the accompanying sketch,[1] taken by the author in July, 1871. Another stone, very similar to these, is situated not many miles distant, at a place known as Music-water.[2] The Nine Maidens (Maiden being doubtless a corruption of Maen) are in this neighbourhood represented, not by a circle as is usually the case, but by nine erect stones, averaging from 11 feet 6 inches to 5 feet 6 inches high, forming an ortholith or single line pointing in a direction N.E. and S.W., and placed at various and unequal distances apart. They are situated on low ground, near the right-hand side of the road

---

[1] See preceding page.

[2] "Musac" is the Cornish equivalent of the highly *unmusical* word "stinking;" Wartha, often changed into "water" is "higher."

leading from St. Columb to Wadebridge. In the same line with these pillars, to the N.E. stands a single rude Menhir, 7 feet 6 inches above ground, and once apparently surrounded by a small circle of stones on edge. This goes by the name of the "Old Man," which, to the believers in the theory of the sun worship, will sound strangely like "Houl Maen" or the "Sun Stone." Indeed, it seems very probable that this stone formed part of the same monument as the Nine Maidens, and that, like many of the circles, a religious, rather than a sepulchral origin, should be assigned it.[1]

A "long-stone" near Mount Charles, St. Austell, is 11 feet 6 inches high; another on the "Long-stone Down," in Sithney, measures eleven feet; and Canon Rogers mentions in a MS. note that "on Molfra Hill, a little below the Cromlech, is a stone fifteen feet long, which seems to have been formerly erect."

Wishing to put beyond dispute the origin and purpose of some few at least of these monoliths, and to ascertain if any were indeed sepulchral, the author recently obtained the requisite permission, and examined the ground round some half dozen of them, which lay conveniently within his reach. From these investigations he obtained the following results:

The first to be explored was one situated in a

---

[1] If Dr. Ferguson makes this monument one of his "acies," no doubt the "Old Man" would be the drill serjeant of the regiment.

valley close to the farm house of Pridden or Penryn, in the parish of Buryan, the property of D. P. Le Grice, Esq., of Trereife, who kindly gave permission for the investigation to take place. This monolith

PRIDDEN STONE.
From a Drawing by the Author.

stands 11 feet 6 inches above the level of the ground, and is only six inches below the surface. It is an extremely rude unhewn mass of granite, tapering slightly towards the top, but nearly twenty feet in girth in the centre. The workman began by removing a hedge which abutted on the southern side, and which it was considered might be the remains of a cairn heaped up against the stone. This impression was confirmed, when, on reaching the natural level of the ground, and removing a thin stone set on its edge against the foot of the pillar, a deposit of splinters of human bone was exposed to view. It was covered by a flat stone only one foot in diameter. Charred wood and a layer of burnt brownish mould accompanied the bones, which, in all, would scarcely have filled a pint and a half measure. No Kist-Vaen had been formed, but the deposit had been placed on the side of a shallow pit, dug to receive the lower end of the "Long Stone," from which it was distant about one foot. The covering stone rested partly on the natural soil, and partly on two small stones which prevented it from crushing the bones. In this instance, the bones were more completely splintered than in any subsequent discovery, the average length of them being less than an inch, and the amount of burning they received must consequently have been considerable. This discovery was made on the 11th of February, 1871.

About half-a-mile to the westward of this stone stands another, thirteen and a half feet in height; three feet being buried in the ground. It stands on the summit of a hill on the farm of Trelew. On the 7th of March a pit was sunk on the north side of this stone, which is quite as rude as the last, but much heavier at the upper end than the lower, a circumstance which causes it to lean towards the southward. Three feet below the surface of the field (for there was no mound), lay a deposit of splintered bones similar in quantity and appearance to that found at Pridden. The splinters in this case were so strongly cemented together that the workman declared they were set in lime. Among them were found charred wood, a small chip of flint subjected to great heat, and a piece of very rudely baked clay, of a reddish colour, two inches in diameter, and shaped like a stopper or plug. The deposit was three feet distant from the base of the pillar; a good deal of fine clay surrounded the bones, but they were protected by no side or covering stone, and, as in the previous instance, had been placed in the side of the pit excavated to receive the monolith.

A precisely similar discovery, namely, that of bone chips and ashes, was made some years since by a labourer while digging "for treasure," by the side of a third rude menhir, about a mile distant from that at Trelew. It is a pyramidal stone, 10 feet 9 inches in height, standing on the estate of Trenuggo, on the right-hand side of the road leading from Penzance to the Land's End, and just inside the hedge. According to the information of the labourer, the pillar was sunk four feet in the ground. Nothing remarkable was found with the bones.

The most important discovery, however, of incinerated remains at the foot of an obelisk, was made in the year 1840, by the tenant at Tresvenneck, in the parish of Paul. The monument in this case is placed on the summit of elevated ground, about a mile and a half to the south-east of the Trenuggo Stone, while the estate on which it is situated joins that of Trigganeris, where the two menhirs with a grave between them, previously described, are situated. The height of the Tresvenneck pillar, a sketch of which is here

TRESVENNECK PILLAR.
From a Sketch by the Author.

inserted, is 11 feet 6 inches above ground, and about four feet below. The stone itself, which, like the others, is granite, seems to have been selected with considerable care. It presents a much more symmetrical appearance than any of those just described, being perfectly upright, and tolerably well squared at the angles, though seemingly unhewn.

The farmer, while engaged in turning up that portion of his field which, from its proximity to the pillar, the plough could not reach, struck his tool against a flat block of stone, eighteen inches square, lying in a horizontal position, at the distance of about two feet from the eastern side of the pillar. This stone being turned up, a pit was discovered, cut out of the solid clay soil, and unprotected by side stones or walling of any description.

In the centre of this pit stood an urn, the largest

TRESVENNICK URN,
From a Photograph.

Large Urn ...... Height .... 19 2-5ths inches.
                 Width at mouth .. 14 3-10ths ,,
Small ,, ... Height .... 5½   ,,
                 Width at mouth .. 4   ,,

perfect one yet found in Cornwall, and belonging to a type of sepulchral vessels which must be noticed more fully at a subsequent page. It stood with the mouth upwards, and contained the larger fragments of the calcined bones of a human body, among which was a molar tooth; while the smaller and more splintered pieces, together with wood ashes, were scattered throughout the rest of the pit. The vessel is formed of yellowish clay, obtainable in the vicinity; it is hand-made, and the exterior scarcely sufficiently baked. The interior on the contrary is hard and blackened by fire, the ashes having been doubtless swept into it, while still red hot, and left to smoulder within. The handles, (a common feature in Cornish urns,) are in this instance remarkably large, and neatly put on; but one, as will be seen, differs from the other in shape and size.

The small urn, which accompanies the large one in the above cut, was found 18 inches to the N.E. of it. It was also standing on its base, without a covering stone or protection of any sort. The mouth is in consequence much broken. It was filled with snuff-coloured powder. The Penzance Natural History and Antiquarian Society, among their many obligations to that gentleman, owe a special debt of gratitude to J. N. R. Millet, Esq., of Bosaverne, for the preservation of this interesting relic; and no less so to those ladies who took infinite pains to restore the urn to its original form, from the countless fragments into which it had been broken.

These four well authenticated discoveries will be sufficient to show the sepulchral character of some at least of the Western "Menhirion." Some, however, belong to a different class, and are either memorial stones "set up for a witness" of some great event or notable compact, or have borne their part in forming one of those inexplicable combinations of standing stones, miniature Aburys and Carnacs, the object and meaning of which still lies as deeply buried as ever under the Stygian darkness of ages out of number.

Three rude pillars which seem to belong to this latter class were explored by the author on the 11th of March, 1871. All three lay within a few hundred paces of the stone circle of Rosemoddress, in the parish of Buryan, a district most fruitful in pre-historic remains.[1] The two taller ones, called the Pipers, and measuring respectfully 15 feet and 13 feet 6 inches in height,[2] are perhaps the finest monuments of the kind in Cornwall. They are eighty-five yards apart, and point in a direction N.E. and S.W. If this line were continued for 260 yards beyond the shorter pillar towards the S.W., it would be found, after crossing the brow of a hill, to bisect the circle of nineteen

---

[1] For a plan of these remains see subsequent page.
[2] Under the turf they are respectively 5 feet, and 1¼ foot.

stones, called the Nine Maidens. Three or four hundred yards due west of this same circle stands the third pillar, 10 feet 6 above the ground, and six inches below. In appearance it is much more slim and tapering than "the Pipers." It stands in a hedge adjoining the "Goon Rith" or Red Downs, a name which has been thought to lend some probability to the tradition of the place, that a great battle was once fought there.

On digging carefully round each of these stones nothing remarkable was discovered, and as menhirs are frequently found in other parts of the British Isles in close proximity to stone circles,[1] the author concludes that they are in this case, as in others, some integral part of the monument, the object of which is unknown.

THE TREGIFFIAN BARROW.

Being unsuccessful in his exploration of the menhirs at Rosemoddress, and having the best part of the day before him, the author directed the workman to a barrow, seemingly less dilapidated than others in the neighbourhood, which stood by the side of the road, some 250 yards to the westward of the

---

[1] Not to go out of Cornwall for instances: there are two pillars (nine feet apart) some 120 feet from the three stone circles, called the Hurlers, near Liskeard; a rude pillar once stood, if it is not standing now, near the circle of Boscawen Un, in the parish of Buryan.

stone circle, and 70 or 80 south of the last mentioned pillar. Here he was fortunate enough to discover a very interesting example of early incinerated interment; which, from the fact that a prostrate menhir lay within a few feet of it, may most properly be inserted in this place.

The turf from the top of the mound being removed, it became quite evident that it had been overhauled before; stones had been taken from it to make the surrounding hedges, and their place supplied by a pile of mud and refuse from the road. Owing to this, the diameter of the barrow could not be ascertained, although, in several places, stones on edge seemed to have formed a rude ring round it. Two feet from the western edge the workman came to a large stone, lying in an inclined position, nine feet in diameter, and eighteen inches thick. The upper and under faces of this stone were flat, and it rested at the south and west sides upon two upright stones, a cavity being thus formed beneath it some two or three feet in depth. The other end rested on the ground, having apparently been knocked off its supporters by a "Long Stone" (eleven feet in length) which had fallen across it. This stone was very similar in character to that in the neighbouring hedge at Goon Rith, and, judging from its present position, the author believes that it once stood upright on the summit of the tumulus, side by side with the Kist-

Vaen. A monument would thus have been constructed precisely similar to those raised by the Khasias in India, of which Dr. Hooker has recently presented the Archæological world with such capital illustrations. Instances of monoliths in close proximity to, or even standing on tumuli are by no means uncommon—one in especial of considerable height, now covered with Christian devices, crowns a large tumulus in the neighbourhood of Carnac.

But to return to the exploration. On the upper face of the covering stone, and probably disturbed before, though never by Archæologists, lay a great quantity of ashes and splintered bones. Among these was found a flint flake, two and a half inches long, excessively sharp, and conveniently formed for handling as a cutting tool. Though of the very rudest, and what would be called the most primitive type of "flint chip," the edges of this instrument

FLINT FLAKE FROM BARROW NEAR ROSEMODDRESS.

seem to bear the unmistakeable marks of use; small scratches or chippings being visible, which are apparently not natural to the stone.[1]

---

[1] So very artificial did these markings at first sight appear, that in revi-

On digging under the covering stone, a very considerable quantity of bone splinters, mingled with ashes, was brought to light; and under a smaller flat stone, placed beneath the southern end of the large one, was found an entirely separate, and more carefully arranged deposit. The small pit in which it was placed was lined with shell sand peculiar to the Cove of Porthcurnow (not the nearest cove), some three or four miles distant, and the bone chips and ashes it contained would more than have filled a quart measure. More than one body was therefore in all probability interred in this barrow. Several pebbles were found in the course of the work, and a round flint, but no trace of pottery or metal. This is rather remarkable in connection with the circumstance that pottery similar to that found with the bronze daggers, has been taken from a barrow quite as near as this one to the circle of Rosemoddress.

---

sing his MS., the author has allowed the above sentence to stand. A communication, however, kindly sent him by Nicholas Whitley, Esq., F.M.S., the author of several most valuable papers on "flint flakes" and the "glacial action," to whom he referred this specimen, seems to set the matter at rest. That gentleman observes "I have examined under a lens the flint flake, and compared it with several shattered flints and ground celts. From the position in which it was found, I should infer that it had been placed there by man. The markings on one of its sides appear to me to be the result of fracture and not made by grinding or use. I find very similar lines on accidentally broken flints, radiating in the same manner from the bulb, and having a shattered look. To illustrate this, I send you a flake crushed out by Blake's Stonebreaker. I observe that the lines on both flints are on the bulb side of the flakes. The lines which result from grinding have a parallelism and a grooved appearance unlike those on your flint."

Before proceeding to relate other instances, where cremation in its simplest form (that is, without pottery or metal) has been discovered by barrow diggers, it may be as well to make a short classification of the various kinds of tumuli which are to be met with in Cornwall.

"The raising of mounds of earth or stone, over the remains of the dead, is a practice," says Mr. Akerman, "which may be traced in all countries to the remotest times." Dr. Wilson adds, that "their origin is to be sought for in the little heap of earth displaced by interment, which still to thousands suffices as the most touching memorial of the dead." It will be superfluous therefore to call to mind the individual instances of this practice which history supplies, or to dwell on the memorials which the conjugal affection of Semiramis, or the vast riches of Crœsus, the friendship of Alexander, or the stern obedience of Joshua to the will of the Deity, raised to the honour or dishonour of the noted dead. From times so remote one might, indeed, pass to European examples of much more recent date, and relate how Sigurd Ring, in the 8th century, buried his vanquished uncle in a tumulus, after the battle of Braavalla, or how Queen Thyra and King Gorm in the middle of the 10th century were interred in a similar manner at Jellinge. Coming nearer home, Mr. Petrie might be quoted for the record of many an ancient

Irish chieftain's burial mound; and lastly, to make the chain perfect down to the present day, one might turn to the American Indians for a similarity in their customs of mound-building, which, when compared with those of ancient Europe, is certainly most remarkable.

Suffice it, for the present, to say, that as far as Cornwall is concerned, not a single record or available tradition, as to the origin of these mounds, has been handed down to us; although by hundreds they lie scattered through the length and breadth of the country; on the summit of almost every hill, along the edges of the cliffs; wherever, in short, a barren tract of country has afforded them protection from the plough.

In the West the word "burrow" (the more correct pronunciation of the usual term barrow,) is applied as well to the refuse heap from the mine, as to the sepulchral mound of more ancient date. In this latter sense it has taken the place of the Celtic "cruc," or vulgarly "creeg," the genuine Cornish word for a hillock or mound, still found among others in the following local names: "Creegcarrow"—Deer's barrow; "Creeglase"—Green barrow; "Cruk heyth"—Barrow-heath; Crig-an-bargus—"Kite's barrow;" and "Creggo" (the plural) "The Barrows." The later Saxon word occurs in Hensburrow, Four-Burrow, &c.

The ancient burrows are sometimes piles of earth,

sometimes accumulations of stones. In the latter case they are termed "cairns," or by the Cornish "Karns."[1] Those tumuli, on the other hand, which are composed of earth and stones indiscriminately thrown together, are seldom or never found to be sepulchral in their origin, but have been raised for a beacon, or occasionally for a hermitage[2] to be perched on their summits. It must be mentioned, however, that in the centre of an earthen barrow, a "cairn" of loose stones[3] is very frequently found. In one instance where this arrangement had taken place, (a most promising barrow on the Carnecledgy Downs near the Nine Maidens, St. Columb,) no interment could be discovered, though the mound was clearly undisturbed by previous explorers.

In spite of Dr. Wilson's opinion to the contrary, as regards Scotland, it may be laid down as a general rule in the case of Cornish "burrows," that those formed of earth belong to districts where stone is not readily obtained, while the "cairns" are the natural product of a stony district. Thus, to the St. Columb,

---

[1] The name Karn, however, belongs to natural as well as to artificial piles of rock and stones, and is frequently applied to the rude formations of granite which protrude through the moors.

[2] Chapel Karn Brea, in St. Just.

[3] In many parts of England this arrangement is the rule and not the exception. Near Winchester, the author discovered burnt bones, and a bone pin under a pile of flints in the centre of an earthen barrow.

St. Austell, and Lizard districts the earthen barrows belong; while "cairns" are invariably found on the granite hills of Dartmoor; at Sharpy Tor, near Liskeard; as well as throughout the entire range of West Cornwall.

By far the greater number of Cornish tumuli, whether cairns, or barrows of earth, were surrounded by circles of stones set on their edge, not peristaliths or rings of rude pillars apart from the mound, like that at New Grange, but circular base-works or walling; the stones being generally contiguous, and serving both to confine the earth or stones within their proper area, and to support the superstructure of the tumulus.

Sir J. Gardner Wilkinson, in his valuable essay on the "British Remains on Dartmoor," states that he discovered at Hayter Tor "concentric-circle-cairns," that is, cairns not only surrounded at the base, but also crowned with standing stones. The extreme desolation of the tract of country in which these remains occur has no doubt preserved in their integrity many a type of monument, which, in more cultivated Cornwall, has lost its characteristic traces; and it is therefore highly probable that the antiquary might once have added this latter class to his list of West Country tumuli.

This ring of stones round the "cairn" formed, as will be presently seen, one of the principal features, and perhaps the first step in the ceremony of the interment.

A Danish Antiquary has attributed those tumuli encircled by great stones to a more primitive age than those not so surrounded.[1] This may be true as far as regards his own country; but in Cornwall, in those few instances where no such circle seems to have existed, interments have been found of a very primitive character, while, on the other hand, in the case of encircled barrows and cairns, discoveries have been made of comparatively recent date. No such distinction is therefore possible, and, indeed, in many cases where no circle appears at first sight, a small amount of digging round the edge of the mound will show that it is really there, and only concealed by an inch or two of turf.

The sepulchral mounds of Cornwall, whether of earth or stones,[2] range from fifteen to one hundred feet in diameter, and from two to twenty-five feet in height. As it has been usual to classify them according to their form, the reader may learn that he will find in Cornwall—first, the Cone-shaped barrow;

---

[1] Worsaae. *Prim: Ant: of Denmark.* Translated by Thoms, p. 93. "The tombs of the stone-period are peculiarly distinguished by their important circles of stones. * * * * * Those of the bronze-period, on the other hand, have no circles of massive stones."

[2] Some cairns are quite as large as the earth-barrows; one on Caradon hill measures even now seventy feet in diameter.

second, the Bowl-barrow; third, the Bell-barrow; fourth, the Flat-barrow; and fifth, the Ring-barrow; a class which may perhaps, with equal propriety, be called the Unfinished barrow.

"Long barrows," "Druid barrows," "Egg barrows," "Twin barrows," (*i.e.*, two surrounded by the same trench,) are unknown.

1. *The Cone-shaped Barrow.* It is probable that all the circular tumuli which had any pretension to height were originally finished, or intended to be finished, by a peak or cone at the top. The action of rain upon this peak of newly formed ground, and doubtless, in many cases, the hollow nature of the centre of the mound itself, caused most invariably a sinkage to take place resulting in a circular depression of the summit. From the form thus acquired the name of Bowl-barrow has been given, as we shall presently see, to these mounds; but there still remain examples where, owing to circumstances, such as the existence of a Kist-Vaen near the summit,[1] such a sinkage could not have taken place; and it is to such as these that the term Cone-shaped barrow is applied. As an example of this form of structure, the reader is here presented with a sketch of the Northern and perfect side of the chambered

---

[1] Dr. Borlase, in the *Ant. of Cornwall*, gives an engraving of a barrow with a Kist-Vaen at the top. When perfect, this was, doubtless, a cone-barrow.

tumulus near Chapel Euny, previously described at page 56.

NORTHERN VIEW OF THE CHAPEL EUNY BARROW.
From a Sketch by the Author.

The elevation of the central chamber, and the small space intervening between the stones that form it, and the ring of upright blocks which support the sides of the mound, render, in this case, the conoid shape unavoidable; and, so thin is the coating of rubble which at present covers the roofing stone, that it is remarkable that neither the action of rain nor the hands of the curious have entirely denuded the chamber long ere this, and reduced it to the same naked state in which nine-tenths of the Cromlechs of the Kist-Vaen type appear. It has been already observed that the greater portion, if not all, of the monuments of this type were once enclosed in tumuli. Where, however, traces of such mounds still remain, as in the instance at Chapel Euny, it does not seem that the area enclosed was of greater extent than barely to admit of the central chamber being thinly covered in by a mound of a sharp conoid shape. If, then, it was by such scanty mounds, with sides nearly perpendicular, that the Cromlechs of the Kist-Vaen type were originally covered, it is not hard to understand how the huge stone chamber quickly came to shake off its inadequate envelope, and emerge once more into the light of day.

In one or two instances the author has observed an attempt to preserve the conoid shape of the stone cairn by covering it with layers of stones on their flat, in such a manner as that each layer should overlap the one below it, in the manner of a Beehive Hut. These instances are rare, and will be adverted to at a future page.

2. *The Bowl Barrow.* This is by far the most usual type of burial mound in the west, as indeed it is in other districts. The name has been given from its resemblance to an *inverted* basin or bowl, the likeness rendered more complete by the slight concavity (previously accounted for) in its summit, corresponding to that caused by the rim round the bottom of the basin. In cairns and earth-barrows this depression is alike observable, though more so in the latter than the former.

3. *The Bell Barrow* is a more lofty variety of

the Bowl Barrow. The name is also given in respect of its shape, a gradual acclivity at the base becoming steeper as it approaches the summit, and giving it the form of a Bell. This form is, perhaps, the natural result of its more lofty proportions, the materials for the upper part having been carried over the new made ground which formed the base. A fine example of a Bell-shaped barrow stands on the summit of the cliff at Trevalga, near Newquay, but the form is decidedly very uncommon in Cornwall.[1] A slight depression is generally found at the top. No cairns of this shape are known.

4. *The Flat Barrow* is a second variety of the Bowl Barrow, and might quite as appropriately be compared to an inverted saucer. It is sometimes scarcely two feet in height, though its diameter is often considerable. It frequently accompanies the higher Bowl Barrows in the lines of tumuli which stretch across the downs, and in more than one instance is found in close proximity to the Cromlech. The Flat Barrow does not appear to be so necessarily surrounded with a ring of stones, as is the higher Bowl Barrow. Cairns in this form are common.

Two barrows, a large and small one, are not unfrequently placed close together. This arrangement

---

[1] About a mile and a half to the East of Bedruthan Steps, along the coast, is a depressed example of a Bell Barrow, surrounded by a slight circumvallation.

is so common in Orkney, that Dr. Wilson believes they "have more than an accidental relation to each other."

It may be here mentioned that from the external form of the Cornish barrow, it is at present impossible to judge of the nature of its contents; though from future investigations the author does not despair of being, to some extent, able to do so.

5. *The Ring Barrow.* Before taking into consideration that class of remains to which this term has been applied, it may be as well to say a few words on the subject of Stone Circles in general. As in the case of the Cromlechs, so in that of the Circles, two pretty well defined varieties are noticeable. 1. Where the stones stand *upright* on their end; are placed at some distance from each other; and enclose only a *level* piece of ground. 2. Where the stones are set *on edge*, (rarely on end); are contiguous to each other; and enclose either a large rock, a few small mounds, or at all events an area of *uneven* ground. These latter are of a smaller size than those of the first class, are undoubtedly sepulchral, and are what will here be termed the "Ring" or "Unfinished Barrows." Dr. Borlase has added a third class of circle very similar in construction to these last; but as they are evidently the bases of huts or pens, they do not belong to the present subject.

1. The district chosen for the subject of these pages presents us with numerous instances of Circles

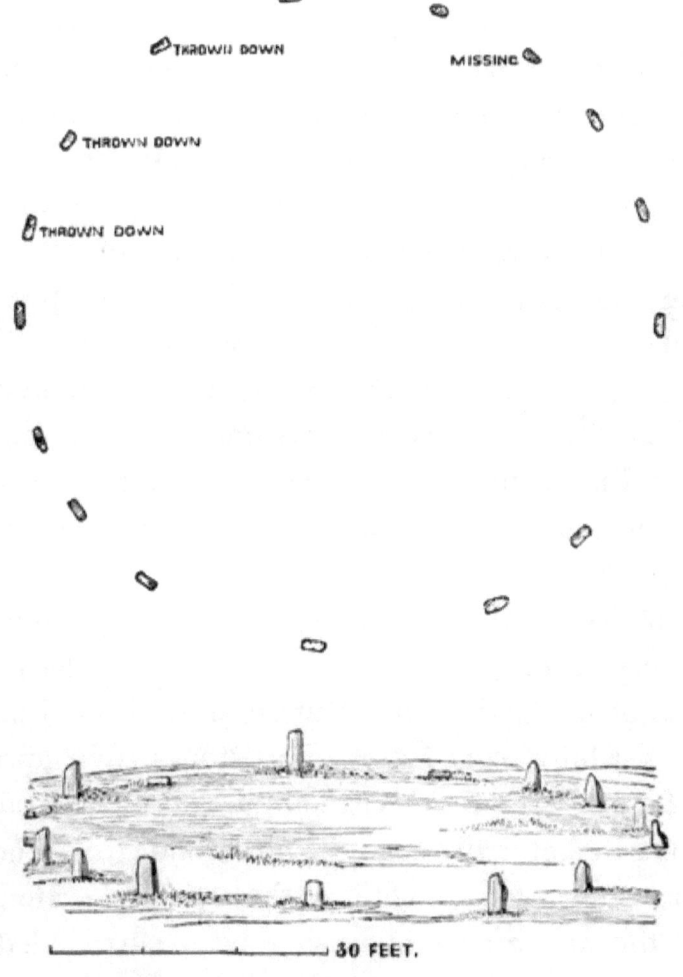

TREGASEAL CIRCLE, ST. JUST.
From a Drawing by Mr. Barnicoat.

of erect stones. Four distinct monuments of this kind are still to be found within a circuit of eight miles in the Hundred of Penwith. They are situated respectively at Boskednan, in Gulval parish; at Tregaseal, in St. Just; and at Rosemoddress and Boscawen-ûn, in Buryan. In all these cases, as Borlase observes, the number of standing stones was nineteen, while the diameter ranges from sixty-eight to seventy-five feet. Of "The Hurlers," (three circles in a line close to Railway Village, near Liskeard,) the centre one has a diameter of 130 feet, while the two others are as nearly as possible equal, their diameters being each 104 feet. The spaces intervening between the centre circle, and that on either side of it, are from seventy to eighty feet. The respective numbers of stones in each ring, as given by Borlase, are sixteen, seventeen, and twelve.

Sir John Maclean, in his valuable work on the Deanery of Trigg Minor, mentions two Circles in the parish of Blisland. One of these, situated on a moor, near Carbilly, consists of nine stones, five upright and four prostrate. It is called the "Trippet Stones," and is 108 feet in diameter. The second circle, known in the reign of Elizabeth as the "Stripple Stones," "has the appearance of having been surrounded by a trench, with an entrance on the east side." Five stones are standing, and eight are prostrate, the diameter is 152 feet, and in the centre is a prostrate stone twelve feet long. This last fact is curious in connection with the Boscawen-ûn circle, near the centre of which a similar pillar is still standing.

The remarkable circles once to be seen opposite the Manor House, at Botallack, in St. Just, have been so frequently figured and described,[1] that they need no further comment at present. Their sepulchral origin, though frequently conjectured, has never been proved; and therefore, until further evidence is forthcoming, it would be superfluous to insert drawings of them in an essay devoted to funereal rites and remains.

Wherever circles of stones erect, such as those just described, are to be found, it seems clear that they owe their origin to the same design which attained its perfection in Abury, and finally in Stonehenge. If the former of these monuments may be called the Westminster Abbey of the circle builders, the latter is no less truly their Sir Christopher Wren's St. Paul's. Whether the Cornish circles are compared with Abury or Stanton Drew, Broidgar or Callernish, the antiquary will find the same primitive design which has led eminent architects to recognize "the

---

[1] Drawings or notices of this really mysterious monument, all copied from Dr. Borlase's plan, will be found in *Buller's History of St. Just*, in *Higgins' Celtic Druids*, in *Fergusson's Rude Stone Monuments* (where they are erroneously named Boscawen circles), &c., &c., &c.

A few of the old people, living near, can remember an upright stone or two standing in the croft where they were, but beyond this there is no trace of them whatever.

circular" as one of the three prevailing characteristics by which to distinguish the so-called *Druidical* remains, whether in the Dekhan of India, or on the barren hills of northern Europe. And not only this, but he will not infrequently be astonished to discover some small matter of detail, which seems to bind together by an inseparable link the manners and customs of peoples separated by rivers and mountains, nay even by the ocean itself. The only question now before him, and which he has, if possible, to decide, is how far the British circles, and the Cornish ones especially, can be regarded as *Sepulchral* in their origin or use.

From the great number of barrows, (as for instance, at Stonehenge), which seem invariably to have been congregated round these monuments, it has been forcibly argued that, if not in themselves sepulchral, they were at least centres of deep and superstitious veneration among the inhabitants of the neighbourhood. If those authors who, from Dr. Stukeley to Sir John Lubbock, have considered Stonehenge (and by inference other remains of the like character) as *temples*, are right in their conjecture, it may fairly be supposed that the same reverential custom which induces Christians to lay those near and dear to them in and around the Church of their GOD, may have had its counterpart in the no less affectionate natures of a ruder age— an age, perhaps, when the newborn instinct of religion prompted a superstitious people to approach, for the performance of their most awful rite, as near as possible to holy ground. But whatever may have been the *origin* of the circle of standing stones, history and tradition seem to point rather to a civil than a religious *use* of them. Thus Homer[1] sings :—

> "Κήρυκες δ'ἄρα λαὸν ἐρήτυον. οἱ δὲ γέροντες
> Εἵατ' ἐπὶ ξεστοῖσι λίθοις, ἱερῷ ἐνὶ κύκλῳ.

and to come to more recent times, and to Northern Europe, there is still extant at Solafordna,[2] in Norway, a place of public meeting composed of twenty-four stones erect placed in a circle, and each of them connected with a central stone by a line of smaller ones. As recently as 1349 a court was held "apud stantes lapides de Rane en le Garniach," and thirty years later the son of Robert II. of Scotland, held his court "apud le standard stanys de la Rathe de Kyngucy Estir."[3] Sir John Lubbock, after quoting these latter instances, says : "This comparatively recent use of the stone circles does not enable us to form any opinion as to the purpose for which they were originally intended." Of the Boscawen-ûn Circle, in Cornwall, there is a curious notice con-

---

[1] *Iliad. lib.* 18, 503.
[2] *Waring's Monuments, &c., of Remote Ages,* pl. 35.
[3] *Prehist. Man.* p. 117.

tained in a Welsh triad, the authenticity of which is perhaps greatly supported by this very fact. It is as follows:—" The three Gorsedds of Poetry in the Island of Britain: the Gorsedd of Beiscawen, in Danmonia, the Gorsedd of Salisbury, in England, and the Gorsedd of Bryn Gwyddon, in Wales." From these and many other sources it may be taken for granted that ancient stone circles, whatever they were, have been found to be very convenient spots for public assemblies or private rencontres, from the first dawn of history, down to the luckless meeting of Minna and her pirate lover among the night-shadowed stones of Broidgar.

Those who think they trace the origin of these monuments to the necessity for providing a sufficiently defined area for the popular assembly, would doubtless account for the traces of mortality which lie scattered around them by supposing that the leaders and elders of the council naturally chose for their burial place the scene of their wisdom and power, where after death they might fairly expect their unwritten virtues to be longest held in remembrance.[1]

---

[1] It is worth remarking in support of this idea, that where there was no central pillar, as at Boscawen and the Stripple Stones, there seems to have generally been one stone in the circle, considerably higher than the others, at which the chieftain or principal speaker may have taken his stand.

This is particularly noticeable at the Boskednan and Tregaseal circles in West Penwith.

But whether their origin is sought in the dictates of policy, or religion, their *purely* sepulchral purpose does not seem sufficiently substantiated either by tradition, or investigation.

That interments have not unfrequently been found within their precincts is simply, as was said before, evidence of the veneration in which they were held, so that the discovery of an urn at the foot of any of the pillars, may only mark the place in the assembly occupied by the deceased during life.

Dr. Wilson,[1] in especial, records the fact that close at the foot of one of the monoliths of a circle on the hill of Tuack, in Aberdeenshire, a sepulchral urn was found, twelve inches high, in the usual inverted position.[2] Traces of sepulture have been often found within the areas of Irish circles; one instance alone has, as far as the author can learn, occurred in Cornwall. Mr. Pedlar mentions that in the year 1861 "an attempt was made to set up the fallen stones" of a circle of stones-erect at Duloe;[3]

---

[1] *Prehistoric Annals of Scotland*, vol. i, p. 417.

[2] At Crichie, also in Scotland, a funereal deposit was obtained at the foot of *every* stone in a circle. *Fergusson's Rude Stone Monuments*, p. 75. See also *Id.* p. 264. Since the above pages were written, Dr. Fergusson has propounded his battle-field origin for the circles. This seems curiously borne out by the traditions at Rosemoddress, *vide infra*.

[3] This circle is near Duloe Church, and equally near a hamlet called Stonetown, which derives its name from that or some adjacent monument now destroyed. In size it more nearly resembles some of the sepulchral circles of the second class, being only twenty-five feet in diameter. Mr. Mac Lauchlan,

"when there was found beneath one of them a cinerary urn with its contents."

FRAGMENT OF AN URN, FROM DULOE CIRCLE.

A fragment of this urn the author is, by the kind permission of T. H. Bewes, Esq., enabled here to figure; and in a letter which he received on the subject from N. H. P. Lawrence, Esq., of Launceston, the additional fact is recorded that it was in pulling down a hedge that the interment was discovered. It seems very probable that a portion of this hedge, as is often the case, was in reality a cairn or barrow raised within the circle; in which case, the monument

---

in a paper written in 1846 for the Journal of the Royal Institution of Cornwall, considers that eight stones completed the circle; of these, six or seven are still standing. Near this circle is a manor called "*Tremodret*" (in Domesday), a name singularly like that of *Rosemoddress*. "Mod," and "rhwy" are equally names for "a ring" in Welsh, and "moderuy" is the Cornish for a "bracelet."

would belong to the second class of circles, such as will presently be described.

Dr. Borlase mentions a remarkable feature in the Circle at Boscawen-ûn which seems to have confirmed his opinion that these monuments were originally sepulchral. "There is part of a Cromlêh," he says, "to be seen on the Skirts of Boscawen-ûn Circle." The two stones which led him to this conclusion still remain in their place or near it, midway between two of the pillars which form the ring. Stukeley seems to have been much interested in this discovery, as appears by a letter addressed by him to a brother antiquary, in October, 1749.[1]

There is a circle on the highest part of the mountain called the "Mule," in the parish of Rushen, Isle of Man, the interior diameter of which is forty-six feet, entirely formed of Kist-Vaens, of which about a dozen can still be traced. As a link in the chain of megalithic remains, connecting the Kist-Vaen and the Circle, this monument is most valuable, and Mr. Halliwell justly observes that it is "perhaps the most curious sepulchral monument in Great Britain." Its sepulchral origin is preserved in the

---

[1] "All my studys in antiquity," says Stukeley in this same letter, "have ever had a regard to religion, nor do I think any other studys are worth cultivating, but what have some aspect that way. I am thoroughly persuaded, our Druids were of the patriarchal religion, and came from Abraham. I believe Abraham's grandson helped to plant our island," &c., &c., &c. *M.S. letter.*

Manx name "Rhullick-y-lagg Shliggah," that is, "the grave yard of the valley of broken slates."

This monument, however, cannot be regarded as belonging to the same class as our circles of erect pillars; and, if the stones at Boscawen-ûn be really the remains of a Kist-Vaen, it must be remembered that the circle would have been equally perfect without this addition, which, therefore, like the urn at Tuack might have been in no way connected with the original design of the structure. It may be added that when a trench was cut some years since through the centre of Boscawen-ûn circle, nothing was discovered; a similar cutting made through that in Rolldich, in Oxfordshire, in the last century, was equally unattended with any evidences of sepulchral interment.

The exploration of the tumuli which surround the circles has in Cornwall, as elsewhere, been attended with varied, and, to those Antiquaries who would draw a sharp line between the Stone and Bronze periods, most perplexing results. The discovery of a flint knife among calcined bones near Rosemoddress Circle has already been noticed; as also the fact that in tumuli equally near that circle, urns, such as occur with bronze daggers, have been brought to light. Close to the Boscawen-ûn circle, similar pottery was found, as will be presently seen, and also small globules of bronze among a deposit of calcined bone. Near the Tregaseal circle, on the other hand, Mr. Buller found in a barrow several greenstone celts of the very rudest type.

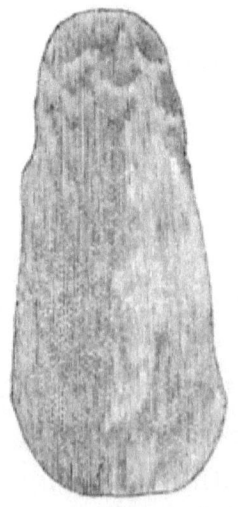 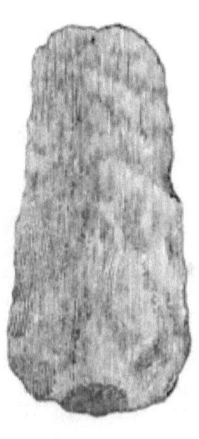

FIG. 1. STONE CELT.   FIG. 2. STONE CELT.
FROM NEAR TREGASEAL CIRCLE.

Of these remarkable implements, two, which are preserved in the Museum at Truro, are here figured.[1] A third is to be found in the Penzance Museum.

With these observations may be dismissed, for the present, the perplexing question of the origin and purpose of circles of stones erect. It must be remembered, however, that in the absence of direct testimony, the antiquary has no more right to call them *purely* sepulchral monuments, than he would

---

[1] Mr. Buller only mentions that they were found in the parish of St. Just, but a labourer supplied the author with the account of their discovery near the "Nine Maidens," at Tregaseal, at which he himself had assisted.

have to apply a similar term to the ruins of Glastonbury Abbey, simply because stone coffins and other indications of interment have been discovered beneath its walls.

We now turn to the second class of circles, or those monuments to which the author has given the name of "Ring Barrows."

2 It is not uncommon, in rambling along the edges of the Cornish cliffs, or over the summit of the uncultivated downs, to stumble upon small circles of earth, or contiguous stones set on their edge. The diameter of these rings ranges from 10 to 100 feet, and their area is occupied either by a few irregular piles of stone, or by a central rock, natural to the surface of the ground. That rings, such as these, were originally sepulchral, there is little doubt; and, on examination, they are almost invariably found to be cairns or barrows in an uncompleted or demolished state.

From the ordinary encircled bowl-barrow take away the superincumbent mound, and you have the ring barrow, with its hearth or burning place and its sepulchral deposit. A remarkable example of one of these remains was explored by Sir Gardner Wilkinson, and by him described and figured in his essay on the British Remains on Dartmoor. It was situated on the Rhôssili Downs, in South Wales, was thirty-three feet in diameter, and very similar in general appearance to the Goonorman circle, figured

SCALE OF FEET

RING BARROW, ON GOONORMAN DOWNS.[1]
From a Sketch by Mr. Barnicoat.

---

[1] The Rev. F. H. A. Wright, vicar of Stithians, has kindly informed me that an urn has recently been discovered "in a small stone chamber," on this same downs.

above. In the centre was an inner circle of contiguous stones, surrounding a hearth "composed of seven flat stones, carefully fitted together, and upon them a mass of charred wood." Below one corner of this hearth was a slab covering a kist in which were fragments of pottery and bones. A pile of stones, 3 feet 4 inches high, had to be removed from this barrow before the hearth was arrived at. In the detailed accounts of the explorations of some Cornish tumuli, presently to be laid before the reader, he will find many instances where, when a few feet of stones or earth have been removed, a natural rock, or altar of incremation, has been discovered standing in the centre of a ring of upright stones. But a ring barrow, properly so termed, seems never to have been covered by a mound at all. Mr. Cotton investigated three of these (26th September, 1826,) with the following results. They lay in the same line, at distances of about 300 feet from each other, on Botrea-hill, in the parish of Sancred. "These circles," he says, "are formed by a low wall or bank of earth and stones, which may be perceived, by some portions remaining, to have been formerly built up in a regular manner, without cement. Their areas are slightly elevated above the level of the ground without (about 18 inches); that towards the south is the most perfect in respect of the size and preservation of its walls; its diameter is sixty feet.

The middle circle is ninety feet in diameter, and the most northern one ninety-eight. The areas of these circles were slightly elevated in three or four places in each, which circumstance induced us to remove the earth from one of them, and we presently came to a small vaulted cell, measuring 3 feet 6 inches long, by two feet wide. It was formed with flat stones, artificially arranged, and covered with a large stone on the top. Within we found a cylindrical earthen pot or urn, about twelve inches in diameter, standing on a slab of granite. On examining the urn, we found it to be made of a coarse kind of clay, mixed with small particles of decomposed granite, very little, if at all, baked; perhaps only burnt in the funeral pile. It contained a rich black earth, unctuous to the touch, and the ashes of burnt wood." It was standing upright, and the upper rim was ornamented with a double border of parallel lines, rudely indented or scratched. "A small flint was found imbedded in the greasy earth within the urn, shaped, and, in size, like a common gun flint. It is probable that it was the instrument used in scratching the ornamental border, as it fits exactly in the marks made on the urn."[1] It was in the most northerly of this same line of barrows that Mr. Cotton discovered

---

[1] *Illustrations of Stone Circles, &c.*, by William Cotton, Esq., M.A., p. 39, *et seq.*

the grave and flint arrow-heads previously described, at page 26.

A short time since, the author caused a smaller ring barrow, about thirty feet in diameter, to be opened on the adjoining hill of Trannack; in this case, the centre was occupied by a large natural granite slab, but no interment could be discovered.

This ring, then, of earth or stones seems to have formed an essential feature in the works of the cairn-builders of the West.

A convenient spot of ground, generally on the bald summit of a hill, was first of all selected as the scene of the funeral solemnity. Where natural rocks, especially of a tabular form, such as the granite often assumes, were found cropping up through the soil, one of them was selected as the most fitting altar upon which to raise the pyre.

ENCIRCLED ROCK AT TRESCAW.

It is highly probable that the Trescaw and Wendron[1] rocks, mentioned and figured by Borlase, and copied by Col. Forbes Leslie into his "Early Races of Scotland," were, in reality, the altars of incremation for the dead; although the circles which surround them have been attributed to idolatrous, rather than funereal customs.

From discoveries made at the Boscawen-ûn, Morvah-hill, and Tredinney Barrows, *(vide infra)*, it is beyond doubt that the central rock often served such a purpose, and was, for this very reason, selected for the ceremony and encircled by the ring.

Where, however, nature afforded the mourners no such substantial bier on which to lay the corpse, a hearth, such as that found at Rhôssili, a pile of stones, or a simple flooring of clay, formed the foundation on which to rest the wood for the burning.

The spot being chosen, the next step seems to have been to surround it by a ring of stones or earth, and thus make it a τέμενος or sacred spot within the precincts of which none might approach who were not engaged in performing the last rites of affection to the deceased, or in kindling and keeping alive the flame. A circle of this kind would be a very useful precaution against the overcrowding of the multitude of spectators who, no doubt, attended at each and all of these funeral rites. It is possible, however, that

---

[1] A drawing of the Wendron rock will be found at a subsequent page.

other and more elaborate ceremonies, some, perhaps, copied from the Romans, actually took place when a great man was to be reduced to ashes. In some cases the barren hills of the west may have even beheld the solemn *Decursio* of the Roman soldiers round the funeral pile :

> Ter circum accensos cincti fulgentibus armis
> Decurrere rogos ; ter mæstum funeris ignem
> Lustravere in equis, ululatusque ore dedisse.

Certain it is that, if the Pre-historic Celts at all resembled their nineteenth-century descendants, in Ireland, Wales, or Cornwall, the funerals of their countrymen were by no means scantily attended. It is, indeed, highly probable that the prevailing habit of flocking from far and near, in their Sunday best, to the funeral of some person with whom, during life, many of them were, perhaps, scarcely acquainted, is attributable quite as much to ancient custom handed down from their ancestors, as it is to the pleasure which the Celtic nature always derives from the contemplation of the melancholy.

The circle being formed, the fire was lighted, sometimes in the centre, sometimes at the side of the area enclosed. Where the body was burnt on a rock, the ashes were swept into a kist or urn at one side of it, but where the pile of wood rested simply on the ground, the charred remains of it are generally to be found on one side of the floor, while the Kist-Vaen is in the centre. In one instance, (a barrow on Boskenwyn Downs, Wendron,) instead of a raised bank of stones or earth being drawn round the area, a ditch was dug three feet deep, at a distance of ten yards from the base of the mound.[1]

The burnt bones being placed in their narrow chamber, and hidden from view, the ceremony was so far completed; and thus what has been termed a "Ring barrow" was formed.[2]

In general, however, the work of barrow building now began, the materials (as has been observed before) depending greatly on the nature of the soil surrounding.[3]

The sketch on next page has been reduced from a drawing made by Mr. Blight, and published in the

---

[1] See plan of this barrow, *Report of the Roy. Institution of Cornwall*, 1862, p. 27.

Another curious barrow, apparently of the same class, is mentioned in *Mr. Davies Gilbert's Historical Survey of Cornwall*, p. 193. "In the midst of an open field, between the villages of St. Erme and Ladock, is a raised circular piece of ground, flat on the top, and secured by a deep ditch. The late Rev. John Collins examined the ground to the depth of several feet, but met with nothing, except ashes, that could elucidate the origin of this rude structure, which from these, was undoubtedly, funereal."

[2] It is very probable that the Senor, or Zennor Circle, of which a drawing is given at Plate xv. of *Borlase's Antiquities*, is nothing more than a "Ring barrow." The stones standing on the top of the circular embankment is an arrangement very similar to that of the Rayne and Fiddes Hill circles in Scotland. In the former of these, Mr. Stuart (*Sculptured Stones of Scotland*, vol. i, p. xxi) discovered ashes, and fragments of urns.

[3] The sentence, "I will add a stone to your cairn," was doubtless quite as proverbial an expression of respect among the Cornu-Britons as it was among the Scotch.

Journal of the Royal Institution of Cornwall, for the year 1867. The "ring" in this case consisted of nineteen or twenty stones, outside which, on the

ENCIRCLED BARROW ON TREWAVAS HEAD.
Denuded of its envelope. (From a Drawing by J. T. Blight, Esq., F.S.A.)

western side, were traces of an outer or protecting ring. The circle was 19 feet 6 inches in diameter, and close to its western side was a Kist-Vaen. The sides of this chamber measured respectively 3 feet 6 inches, and 2 feet 10 inches in length; the height was 2 feet 3 inches. The covering stone measured 4 feet 5 inches long, 4 feet wide, and 1 foot 11 inches thick. The cairn was unfortunately rifled by a miner, with what result is unknown. It is perched, like many others, on the very edge of the cliff, and is an excellent specimen of a type of encircled barrow by no means uncommon in Cornwall. When perfect it probably belonged rather to the Cone-shaped, than to the Ring barrow class,[1] and is only inserted in

---

[1] A very curious example of what, but for its envelope, would have been

this place as a good specimen of the interior of a cairn divested of its superincumbent mound.

In a subsequent part of this essay, several minor details in connection with the ceremony of the interment will be brought to light, such as the positions of the urns, the formation of the kists, and the general structure and design of the mounds themselves. But, meanwhile, two questions, much disputed in the Archæological world, must not be passed by without remark.

Firstly. Is there any good reason to suppose that the articles interred with the deceased were placed there with a view to their utility in the next world; that is, are they the result of a matured belief in a future state? The author must confess at once that he does not believe that their presence there is due to any such feeling. Cornish barrows are, as a general

---

termed a "concentric ring-barrow," is noticed by J. N. R. Millet, Esq., in the *Report of the Royal Institution of Cornwall*, for the year 1840. This structure was discovered on the hill known as Carn Galva, in the parish of Zennor. It consisted of a pile of stones, covering three concentric walls. The inner of these was much decomposed; in the second the stones were much more perfect, and the wall of better workmanship. The third was not so well built as the second, the stones being more rounded by decomposition. At the base of the barrow, black earth was mixed with the stones to the depth of more than a foot, and in the lower part was some charcoal. Between the second and third walls an Urn was found of coarse clay, having on its upper part the common dotted zigzag ornamentation. It was mouth-upwards, and was filled with black earth, charcoal, and burnt bones, "apparently those of a young person."

An engraving at page 451 of *The Rude Stone Monuments*, of the uncovered base of a tumulus at Nikolajew is strikingly similar to this Carn Galva barrow. The one on the Steppes of Asia, the other at the extremity of Britain!

rule, unproductive; and if each object, as the spade brings it to light, cannot be accounted for by accident, it may at least be ascribed to the same affectionate feeling which so often prompts people, now-a-days, to lay beside the departed some trifling object dear to them in life. While, however, the idea is thus negatived in the precise terms in which it has been put, it must not be taken for granted that a belief in futurity was non-existent in the days of the barrow-builders. Indeed, some of these monuments seem to date from an age when it would have been hard to find an educated citizen, or even a rude provincial, in Europe, who was not impressed, either by his religion or his philosophy, with some sort of belief of this kind, no matter how indistinct it might be. But, the bronze dagger, the flint arrow-head, and the charm, are the exception and not the rule in Cornish barrows; and, with the exception of a golden drinking cup, and a few daggers, literally nothing has been found, which could be of the least service to one setting out for the banquets of Valhalla, or the war-trails of the Gods.

In this opinion, viz.: that the relics were merely votive offerings of affection at the tomb, Mr. Greenwell, after his long experience in the primitive graves of the north, fully concurs. There are, however, many advocates of the contrary opinion; and, indeed, it would be the more poetical view of the case were it admissible to sing with Schiller those beautiful lines, so exquisitely translated by Lord Lytton, and quoted by Sir Charles Lyell:—

> "Here bring the last gifts!—and with these
>   The last lament be said;
> Let all that pleased, *and yet may please*,
>   Be buried with the dead.
>
> Beneath his head the hatchet hide,
>   That he so stoutly swung;
> And place the bear's fat haunch beside —
>   The journey hence is long!
>
> And let the knife now sharpened be
>   That on the battle day
> Shore with quick strokes—he took but three—
>   The foeman's scalp away!
>
> The paints the warriors love to use,
>   Place here within his hand,
> That he may shine with ruddy hues
>   Amidst the spirit land."

The second question which remains to be answered is: What evidence, if any, is there in Cornish barrows of the custom of slave-killing, or the suttee? There is indeed none whatever. The only instance that seems at all in point, is that of the barrow near the Rosemoddress Circle, previously described, where the calcined bones certainly represented the remains of several, perhaps a great number of bodies. But, if Dr. Fergusson's battle-field theory be entertained, this fact is thoroughly accounted for. In all other cases, the presence of more than one deposit of ashes in the same tumulus can be amply accounted for, either by secondary interments, or by separate collections of the ashes of the pyre.

A few words on the fictilia of the barrows will close this portion of the subject.

The pottery found in Cornish tumuli does not readily fall into the classification made by Antiquaries for any other part of England. As might be expected, the urns of Devon and Dorset bear the nearest resemblance to it; but with the general type of North-country fictilia it seems to have little in common.

The Larger Cinerary or Sepulchral Urns may roughly be divided into two classes according to their shape—

VASE-SHAPED SEPULCHRAL URN, FROM PENQUITE,
From a Sketch by the late Canon Rogers.

1. Vase-shaped vessels, averaging ten to twenty inches in height, ribbed with bands or ridges round the upper part, sometimes ornamented with small indentations, but never with the chevron or dansette pattern.
2. Cylindrical or Barrel-shaped vessels, averaging from eight to thirteen-and-a-half inches in height, invariably ornamented with the chevron pattern.

Besides these, however, smaller vessels, which, from their resemblance to the larger ones, may be

CYLINDRICAL URN, FROM LANLAWREN,
From a Sketch by Mr. Couch.

termed "Miniature Sepulchral Urns," are very frequently found in Cornish barrows. These are sometimes found standing in close proximity to the larger

K

urns, (in which cases they are unquestionably intended for miniature representations of them),[1] but not uncommonly by themselves. They average from four-

MINIATURE URN,
"Dug up on an estate of Sir John St. Aubyn, west of Penzance, containing human ashes."
From a Drawing by the late Canon Rogers.
Height and diameter .... 5 inches.

and-a-half to six inches in height. As they generally *contain* a considerable quantity of burnt bones, mixed with snuff-coloured powder and ashes, these Miniature Urns[2] cannot come under Mr. Bateman's definition of *Food Vessels*, nor do they agree any better with that gentleman's description of Incense Vessels, or Drinking Cups. Of the former, viz., Incense Cups, there are no examples in Cornwall; and, of the

---

[1] See Tresvenneck and Trevello Urns, at a previous page.
[2] Some Antiquaries suppose them to be children's urns. One is said to have occurred in Scotland, where the bones were identified as those of an infant.

Drinking Cups, only one or two exceedingly doubtful instances can be adduced. A cup, found by the author, at Denzell Downs, near St. Columb is, perhaps, the best authenticated example of this class, but even this curious little vessel does not resemble the "Drinking Cup" known to the Antiquary of the North; and, more than this, it may be considered as a genuine cinerary urn, inasmuch as it *contained* calcined bones.

A vessel much more resembling the shape of Mr. Bateman's "Drinking Cup" is the "Sancred Urn," figured in Borlase's Antiquities of Cornwall, and reproduced at a subsequent page. But even in this case, it was in company with "well-burnt ashes."

"In a barrow, on Lamburn Downs, in the parish of Piran Sanz," says Hals, "was found an earthen pot, containing about two gallons, wherein was lodged much ashes, some bones in small pieces, and charcoal; and, by the side of the said pot, were also found two small drinking cups of like clay, with several handles made of the same matter." As, however, this good old Cornish Antiquary did not live in the "Drinking Cup" age, it is impossible to decide what sort of vessels these were.

The almost universal prevalence of handles, from the rudest unpierced cleat, down to the well-formed pitcher handle on Cornish pottery, is very remarkable.

No extant example of Cornish fictilia has been found with unburnt bones.

The texture of the sepulchral urn is, in general, rude in the extreme, and the baking on the exterior of the vessel exceedingly slight. In the case of several fragments in the author's cabinet, the soft yellow clay which forms the outer coat has scarcely lost its original consistency, while the hard black lining of the interior of the vessel, has evidently been subjected to great and continued heat. This fact has already been noticed in connection with the Tresvenneck Urn, and doubtless arises from the ashes of the pyre having been deposited in it while yet red hot.

On comparing the pottery taken from the tumuli, with that found in the British huts and Cave dwellings, it becomes evident that while the former was made on the spur of the moment, to contain (according to custom) the remains of the dead, and then be lost sight of for ever, the latter was formed for lasting and continuous use. The domestic ware was so constructed as to contain water within, at the same time that it was subjected to the action of fire without. Thus we find it to be thick, hard, and at times slightly glazed. The clay, however, of which it is composed, is precisely the same as that of the sepulchral urn; and where ornamentation is attempted, (which is seldom,) it is the same chevron pattern,[1] occasionally relieved by rows of indentations, the product of the end of a stick, or perhaps of an implement of flint, bone, or bronze.

Some specimens of the pottery from the ancient British dwellings bear evident marks of having been made on a wheel of some kind. How far true it would be to venture a similar statement with regard to the urns, is a question very difficult to decide. That those of the cylindrical shape, and chevron pattern, are exceedingly symmetrical, no one can doubt who will turn to the engraving of the Trevello Urn; and it seems really beyond belief that so rude a process as that mentioned by Messrs. Squier and Davis, namely, the stick and hand, should be imported into Britain by our Archæologists to account for the formation of vessels so well fashioned, and so accurately finished, as the urns of this description usually are.

With regard, then, to the cylindrical urns at least, the author is of opinion that a wheel of some description was used in their formation; although, in the case of these vessels, it was seldom or never thought necessary to bring the clay to that state of maturity and thickness necessary for domestic use.

---

[1] Two specimens of the chevron pattern on domestic pottery have come respectively from "Roman" remains at Carminow, and from Carne, in Zennor. A good specimen of the indented pattern was found with Samian ware, &c., in a subterranean dwelling at Chapel Euny.

As a rule, the urns display far greater ornamentation than the domestic pottery; but they are carelessly baked, and their shape is, (seemingly, according to custom,) one peculiarly their own. There is nothing, therefore, in the fictilia itself, to shew that some of these urns may not contain the ashes of the dwellers in the huts and caves.

The reader having thus become acquainted with the various classes of sepulchral remains he may expect to meet with in Cornwall, it now remains to collect from the county histories and MSS., as well as from the author's own notes, such detailed accounts of the explorations of the tumuli, as still lie within reach of the Archæologist.

It may be said, that in bringing evidence to bear on these subjects, nothing should be adduced but the author's own experience in barrow digging, or those facts which have been elicited during the last few years by persons conversant with the modern scientific view of the matter. This view is, in great measure, correct. Few persons have the faculty of careful observation, still fewer that of careful relating. Ask a labourer, a week or two after he has made some discovery, to give you an account of it, and you will soon see how much exaggeration has effected in the meantime. Still, as regards Cornwall, so little has been recorded, and alas! so very little still remains to be explored, that surely it will be pardonable to pick up every scrap of information, and let the reader himself judge of its value. Take, for instance, a passage from Carew, who wrote in 1602. " I haue receiued," says he, " credible information, that some three yeeres sithence, certaine hedgers deuiding a closse on the sea side hereabouts, (*i.e.*, Trewardreth Bay), chanced, in their digging, vpon a great chest of stone, artificially joyned, whose couer, they (ouer-greedy for booty) rudely brake, and therewithall a great earthen pot enclosed, which was guilded and graued with letters, defaced by this misaduenture, and ful of a black earth, the ashes (doubtles) as that, the *urna*, of some famous personage." Now, let there be deducted from this the pardonable "gilding," which three years had given to the story; let the chevron pattern be substituted for the letters; and the reader can make the rest of the narration thoroughly consistent with hundreds of other discoveries, and doubtless with the facts of the case. It is therefore with the intention of giving the reader all the information he possibly can, where inductive evidence is so slight, that the author has added to his own scanty list of researches the accounts contained in the works of those who have preceded him.

Explorations & Discoveries in the Tumuli.

"O for a stroke of luck like his, who found
A crock of silver, turning up the ground."

     Horace, Sat. vi.   Transl. *Conington.*

THE ONE[1] BARROW. ST. AUSTELL DOWNS.

[From the account given in Mr. Whitaker's *Cathedral of Cornwall*, vol. ii., p. 83.]

"In the middle of that extended waste, the downs of St. Austle, was, what was called, One Barrow. This waste, in 1801, was resolved to be enclosed, and the barrow was obliged to be levelled. In this operation, the single workman came near the centre, and there found a variety of stones, all slates, ranged

---

[1] Probably "wyn," Welsh "gwyn" white—white barrow. "*One* man" is the name of a cairn at Moytura.—See Fergusson's *Rude Stone Monuments.*

erect in an enclosure nearly square. The stones were about one foot-and-a-half in height, apparently fixed in the ground before the formation of the barrow. The stones were all undressed, but had little stones carefully placed in the crevices at the joints of the large, in order to preclude all communication between the rubbish without and the contents within. On the even heads of these stones was laid a square freestone, which had evidently been hewn into this form, which seemed to rest with its extremities on the edges of the others, and was about eighteen or twenty inches in diameter. The summit of the barrow rose about eight or ten feet above all. In the enclosure, the leveller found a dust, remarkably fine, and seemingly inclining to clay. On the surface it was brown, about the middle downwards it took a dark chesnut colour, and at the bottom it approached towards a black. On stirring it up, a multitude of bones appeared, different in the sizes, but none exceeding six or seven inches in length. Among them were some pieces about the largeness of a half-crown, which, from their concave form, convinced him they were parts of a skull. The whole mass of bones and ashes might (he thought) be about one gallon in quantity. On touching the bones, they instantly crumbled into dust, and took the same colour with the same fineness as the dust in which they were found. They were exceedingly white when they were first discovered, but remarkably brittle; the effect assuredly of their calcination in a fire, antecedent to their burial. Much in fineness and in colour with these ashes, appeared several veins of irregular earth on the outside of the enclosure; which, from their position without, yet adjoining, and from the space occupied by them there, he conjectured to have been bodies laid promiscuously upon the funeral pile." Such is Mr. Whitaker's account of the One Barrow. It may be added, that the workman rebuilt the kist-vaen in a hedge adjoining, and deposited in it the bones as he found them.

BARROWS, NEAR LANYON CROMLECH.

[From an account given to the author by Mr. Hitchins, the proprietor of the estate.]

A hundred yards or so to the northward of the Lanyon Cromlech and between that monument and the farm-house, was a barrow some twenty-five or thirty feet in diameter, which, like the "One Barrow," had to be removed for agricultural purposes. During its removal, some four years since, the workmen discovered in the centre a ring of large stones set on edge. In the centre of this ring, and placed on the natural soil, was a large deposit of human bones and charred wood, as much as would fill a four-gallon measure. Among these, Mr. Hitchins noticed a jaw-bone with the teeth still in their places. These relics were again deposited in the place where they were found.

On the South-west side of Lanyon Cromlech, and twenty-one feet distant from that monument, is a long low barrow, which, being opened, was found to contain a ring of stones set on their edge in the centre, in a similar manner to the one just described. The place had clearly been overhauled before, probably on more than one occasion, and nothing remarkable was found.

VERYAN BEACON.

[From an account given by the Rev. J. Adams, in the *Journal of the Royal Institution of Cornwall*, 1855.]

"The Beacon of Veryan stands on the highest ground in Roseland, at a short distance from the cliff which overlooks Pendower and Gerrans Bay.

Its present height above the level of the field in which it stands is about twenty-eight feet, and its circumference at the base 350 feet; but it must have been originally much larger, as a considerable portion on one side has been removed, its summit being now about eighty feet from the base on the south side, and only fifty feet on the north, whilst the top of the cairn which was discovered in it, and which was no doubt placed exactly in the original centre of the mound, is at least ten feet still further north than the present summit.

A tradition has been preserved in the neighbourhood, that Gerennius, an old Cornish saint and king, whose palace stood on the other side of Gerrans Bay, between Trewithian and the sea, was buried in this mound, and that a golden[1] boat and silver oars were used in conveying his corpse across the bay, and were interred with him."

Having obtained the consent of the Rev. S. J. Trist, on whose land it stands, and accompanied by the Hon. and Rev. J. T. Boscawen and other gentlemen, Mr. Adams commenced the excavation on the 8th of November, 1855.

"We began," he says, "by cutting a trench towards the centre, at an elevation of about eight feet above the ground. On the third day of the operation, the workmen came upon the side of a heap of large stones, built up rudely but firmly on one another, at a distance of forty feet from the outside of the cutting. After clearing away as much as possible of the earth from the stones, and digging to the base of the heap, which lay about four feet below the level of the trench, and twenty feet below the top of the mound, we proceeded to penetrate this cairn." A mass of earth here unfortunately fell in,

---

[1] This tradition of a golden boat in connection with a Cornish barrow is rendered doubly curious by a report which seems to have been current at the early part of this century, that a golden boat had been found in a barrow near the Cheese-Wring.

completely overwhelming two of the workmen, and partially interring one or two amateur excavators. The diggers having been in their turn dug out, not much the worse for this accident, "it was thought advisable to clear away all the earth above the stones, before attempting to remove any more of them; accordingly the trench was lengthened, so as to ensure our uncovering the cairn beyond its centre, thus making a cutting altogether sixty-four feet in length, and widening from 3 feet 6 inches on the outside, to nineteen feet at the interior. Immediately above the middle of the cairn, several indications were found of the ground having been disturbed subsequent to the construction of the mound; *e.g.*, the outer coating of rubble, which formed a distinctly marked stratum along the sides of the trench, had been broken through in various places, and as we descended, it became manifest that several narrow shafts had been sunk from the summit of the mound to the central heap of stones; at the bottom of each of these shafts there were ashes, half calcined bones, some of which were identified as human, and a quantity of light-coloured clay."

"In one place the cairn itself had been opened to the depth of three feet, in order to admit the ashes of a funeral pile; and in another, a small cavity, containing ashes and bones, had been carefully formed, and covered with a large flat stone, about two feet wide. In fact, it was evident that the top of the mound had been used as a place of sepulture long after its construction, that in every interment the body had been burnt, and that the ashes had been deposited as near as possible to some sacred remains beneath the cairn; probably they were in some cases enclosed in unbaked clay,[1] as in one of the graves there was a stratum of clay two inches thick, mixed with ashes and charcoal, whilst in others there was no clay whatever, but merely ashes and bones. In removing the cairn underneath these graves, large oblong stones were found, placed erect one above another, from the apex to the base of the pile. They were no doubt so placed, in order that the top of the cairn might be uniformly preserved in its erection, above a certain point beneath. That point, as we conjectured long before we reached it, was the resting place of the ancient king. It consisted of a Kist-Vaen, formed of massive unhewn rocks, lying north and south. Its length was 4 feet 6 inches, breadth two feet, and depth 2 feet 6 inches. The covering slab was a huge limestone rock, nearly two feet thick, and the sides were smooth rocks of the same kind, placed on their edges, and resting on the soil. We removed the south end of the tomb without much

---

[1] This remark probably applies to very many other instances, where pottery is absent.

difficulty, but found nothing whatever within, besides ashes, mixed with small stones, pieces of charcoal, and dust of a brownish hue. The contents were carefully examined, but not the least trace of pottery, armour, or other relics, could be discovered."

For the indefatigable perseverance with which Mr. Adams and his friends carried on the investigation of this extensive tumulus, no less than for the concise and graphic account he has given of the work and its results, he deserved the best thanks, not of Cornish antiquaries only, but of the Archæological world at large.

BARROW AT SAMSON, SCILLY.

[From a paper by Augustus Smith, Esq., read at the Meeting of the Royal Institution of Cornwall, May 29th, 1863.][1]

It will be remembered that at a previous page the reader's attention was directed to a line of long graves, extending along the back of the Southernmost hill on Samson island.

The Barrow, now to be noticed, is situated with four or five others, mostly rifled, on the corresponding high ground at the Northern[2] end.

---

[1] Mr. Smith mentions the remarkable fact that similar grave mounds occur even on those islands which are too small ever to have been inhabited.

[2] It is a characteristic feature in the Isles of Scilly, that the greater number of them are composed of two elevated plateaux of granite, connected by a narrow isthmus of sand.

"The mound, in its outer circumference, measured about fifty-eight feet, giving, therefore, a distance of near upon thirty feet to its centre, from where the excavation was commenced. For about eighteen or twenty feet the mound appeared entirely composed of fine earth, when an inner covering, first of smaller and then of larger rugged stones, was revealed. These were carefully uncovered before being disturbed, and were then one by one displaced till a large upright stone was reached, covered by another of still more ponderous dimensions, which projected partially over the edges of the other. At length this top covering, of irregular shape, but measuring about 5 feet 6 inches in its largest diameter, was thoroughly cleared of the superincumbent stones and earth, and showed itself evidently to be the lid to some mysterious vault or chamber beneath." On the lid being removed, there was "disclosed to view an oblong stone chest or sarcophagus beneath," on the floor of which, "in a small patch," "a little heap of bones, the fragmentary framework of some denizen of earth, perhaps a former proprietor of the Islands—were discovered piled together in one corner."

"The bones were carefully taken out, and the more prominent fragments, on subsequent examination by a medical gentleman, were found to give the following particulars:—Part of an upper jawbone presented the alveolæ of all the incisors, the canines, two cuspids, and three molars, and the roots of two teeth, very white, still remaining in the sockets. Another fragment gave part of the lower jaw with similar remains of teeth in the sockets. All the bones had been under the action of fire, and must have been carefully collected together after the burning of the body. They are considered to have belonged to a man about 50 years of age."

During a subsequent examination of these remains the flint, here figured, was discovered amongst them.

FLINT FROM THE SAMSON BARROW.

"The bottom of the sarcophagus was neatly fitted with a pavement of three flat but irregular-shaped stones, the joints fitted with clay mortar, as were also the interstices where the stones forming the upright sides joined together, as also the lid, which was very neatly and closely fitted down with this same plaster."

"Two long slabs, from seven to nine feet in length, and two feet in depth, form the sides, while the short stones fitted in between them make the ends, being about three-and-half feet apart, and to fix which firmly in their places, grooves had been roughly worked in the larger stones." The paving stones had been "embedded immediately upon the natural surface of the granite of which the hill consists."

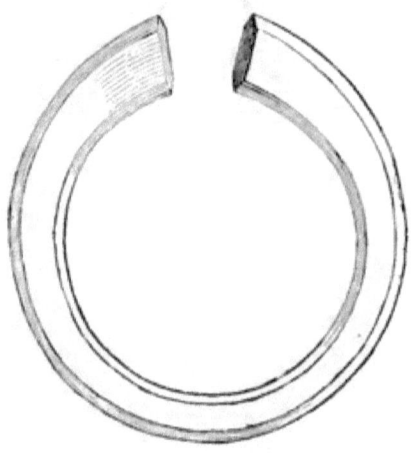

One of two Bronze Armlets, from St. Mary's, Scilly.
Half the actual size.

The above woodcut represents one of two bronze armlets, found about fifty years ago in a barrow on the Peninnis Head, in the island of St. Mary's, Scilly. Their discovery is mentioned in the above paper on the Samson barrow, but under what circumstances it occurred is unfortunately not recorded.

Mr. Smith has generously deposited them both in the Museum at Truro.

Urn Burial.

WITHIEL.

Norden, who is thought to have made his Survey in 1584, records the discovery of an urn in a Cornish barrow. His account is as follows :—" An auntient buriall." "Withiell," a parishe wherin one Gydlye, not manie yeares since, as he was digging a borowe or buriall hill, wherof ther are manie in theis partes, in the time of the Romish, Saxon and Danish warrs occasioned to be made, founde in the bottome of the borow, 3 whyte stones sett triangularly as pillars supportinge another stone nere a yard square, and vnder it a earthern Pott verie thyck, haulfe full of black slymye matter, seeminge to have been the congealed ashes of some worthy man, ther comitted in this manner to his buriall; the like wherof have been, and are often founde."[1] Would that modern antiquaries would be so concise and graphic in their accounts!

TRELOWARREN.

[The following accounts are taken from the printed Works and MSS. of Dr. Borlase.][2]

Ant. p. 214. "In a field at Trelowarren, there

---

[1] p. 70, edit. 1728. Carew, who published his Survey in 1602, gives the same account with the addition that the name of the Barrow was "Borsneenas." See p. 140.

[2] Besides the urns mentioned here, Dr. Borlase found one at, or very near to Castle-an-dinas, no account of which is preserved.

was opened in July, 1751, an Earthern Barrow, very wide in circumference, but not five feet high. As the workmen came to the middle of the Barrow, they found a parcel of stones set in some order, which being removed, discovered a Cavity about two feet diameter, and of equal height. It was surrounded and covered with Stones, and inclosed Bones of all sorts, Legs, Arms, Ribs, &c., and intermixed with them some Wood-ashes; there was no Urn here; but at the distance of a few feet from the central cavity, there were found two Urns, one on each side, with their mouths turned downwards, and small bones and ashes inclosed. All the black vegetable mould which covered the place where the urns were found, was industriously cleared off, and the Urns, inverted, placed on the clean yellow clay (which in this field lies under the soil); then the black vegetable mould was placed round about the urns; and throughout the whole composition of the Barrow, I observed afterwards the same materials, clay, mould, wood-ashes, and rubble-stone, mixed very disorderly, so that there can be no doubt but that the people who formed this Barrow took indifferently of the mould and clay that lay nearest at hand. Three thin bits of brass found near the middle, just before I came there, were given me by the Workmen; they were covered with *ærugo*, neither inclosed in the cavity, nor in the urns, by which I conjecture, that they were pieces of a sword, or some other instrument of war, which, after having been inserted in the funeral pile, and broke, were thrown into the Barrow among the earth, and other materials that were heaped together."

It is much to be regretted that in this instance the Doctor has neither figured the pottery, nor described its shape or ornamentation.

CHIKARN.

Ant. p. 234. "Sometimes * * we find many Urns placed close one to another; the most remarkable Monument of which kind that I have yet heard of in Cornwall, was that opened by Ralph Williams, yeoman, in the tenement of Chikarn, (St. Just, Penwith,) where, (A.D. 1733,) in removing a Barrow, was discovered a great number of Urns; and as they approached nearer the centre, a stone square chest, or cell, paved under foot, in which was also found an Urn, finely carved, and full of human Bones, (as I have been informed, since the death of R. W., by his daughter, who saw the Urn, which her Father brought from the field into his house). As well as could be remembered, (at the time when I had this relation from him, which was four years after the discovery,) there were about fifty Urns which surrounded the central and principal one, which alone, because it appeared to be neatly carved, he carried home to his house, the rest (all which had some remains of bones and earth in them) were thrown away and broke, as of no consequence."

The farm on which this remarkable find took place, lies about four miles from the Land's End, but search has been made in vain to identify the spot on which the barrow stood. On the top of the "karn," or rough hill from which the farm takes its name, stands a large artificial "karn," of the bell shape. On the summit of this, which is some twenty-five feet in height, there once stood an ancient oratory called Chapel Karnbrè. This is now completely demolished. A few years since, the author caused a trench to be dug to the centre of the mound, in hopes of finding a central chamber. Nothing was, however, discovered, and it is possible that the mound was raised merely for the sake of placing the anchorite's habitation (like those of the Egyptian hermits) a few feet nearer to heaven. On the western side of this farm may be observed a track-way, which Dr. Borlase considered as a Roman Road, leading towards the Land's End. A barrow, partially demolished, is contiguous to it on the Northern side.

BOSAVERN RÔS.

Ant. p. 235. There are "three Barrows lying in a line nearly S.E. and N.W., in the tenement of Bosavern Rôs, in the same parish, (St. Just,) about a mile distant from the foregoing. In the easternmost Barrow, about the year 1748, there was found the carcase of a man laid at full length;[1] a long stone on each side, and one at each end on their edge, the cavity like a grave, the bones large sized, no stone covering the body; the middle Barrow was opened afterwards, and bones in it, but not regularly placed; the Barrows seem to have been searched before. On the 29th of May, 1754, I got the westernmost Barrow to be opened; there was a kind of cave or door vault which led into this Barrow, with a tall stone on each side, and a covering stone across, but fallen inside;[2] the floor was riddled clear to the rabman, (or hard ground), on which there was about three inches depth of sea-shore gravel, the biggest of the gravel about three-quarters-of-an-inch diameter, then some bones scattered on the gravel, then an Urn of the contents of three quarts (beer measure) full of bones, and a little partition beyond it fixed on the gravel; about a foot farther, some walling, which, being removed, a little Urn of about a pint full of bones appeared in a cell of stonework, (the cell about 2 feet 8 inches long, and 1 foot 6 inches wide, with a covering flat-stone), placed upon the rabman (no beach or gravel under the Urn); when this little Urn

---

[1] Also mentioned at a previous page.
[2] A curious feature, when compared with the door-ways of the British hut circles.

was taken out, at about a foot distance appeared the side of a tall great Urn, 1 foot 3 inches high, the bottom eight inches wide, of the contents of three gallons and half, full of bones to within three inches of the top; some bones eight inches long, and with the bones several pieces of burnt sticks.

 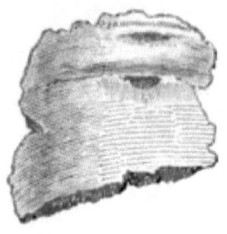

FRAGMENTS OF THE BOSAVERN URN.
From the Engravings in the "Antiquities of Cornwall."

About four inches distant from the great Urn stood two other Urns of about two quarts each, which, with the little one abovementioned, stood triangularly round the great one, which stood in the middle. Matted grass had forced its roots among the bones. The northern and eastern parts of this Barrow consisted of natural rock and ground, not moved since the flood; the rest was artificial, with a ring of rocks forming the outer edge: that part which inclosed the Urns was factitious, and had a wall doubled (*i.e.* faced within and without) of large stones for the space of fifteen yards, about five feet high; the whole Barrow about fifteen feet high, thirty-six feet diameter. Several shreds of Urns were found before they came to the bottom; by which it may be justly conjectured that there were more stages of Urns than one, some placed above the lowermost, when the undermost area was filled." The form of handle figured above is unique in Cornish Urns, the hole being perpendicular, instead of horizontal, as is usually the case.

Mr. Buller (*History of St. Just*, page 90) adds to this account, that about two years before he wrote, (that is in 1840) when "an enclosure was making on the same common, the workmen cut across the remains of an old barrow, and on the level with the surface of the surrounding soil, found three urns of coarse clay which were unfortunately broken, but their contents were nothing more than fragments of calcined bones, and ashes."

GWYTHIAN.[1]

Ant., p. 236. *MS. Par. Mem.*, p. 23. "A remarkable Urn was found in Gwythian parish, where, in May, 1741, about half-a-mile to the S.W. of the Church-town, the sea having washed[2] away a piece of the cliff, discovered (about three feet under the

---

[1] Tradition held that the Castle of King Theodore was on the coast of this parish.

[2] On the 21st of February, 1872, the author noticed several barrows a few miles east of Gwythian Church-town, one of which was standing so close to the edge of the cliff that half it had already slipped away.

On the Reskajeage Downs are five large barrows, all of which seem to have been opened.

common surface of the land) a small cavity about twenty inches wide and as much high, faced and covered with stone.

GWYTHIAN URN, AND KIST.
From an unpublished Drawing by Dr. Borlase.

Height by scale... .... 10¾ inches.

The bottom was of one flat stone, and upon it was placed an Urn with its mouth downwards, full of human bones of which the vertebræ were very distinct. Round about the Urn was found a quantity of small dust or earth, which had all the appearances of human ashes, (in the opinion of Mr. Treweeke, Surgeon, of Penzance, to whom the Urn was brought on the 5th of June.) and filled the lower part of the cavity about four inches high from the bottom."

The above drawing is taken from the sketch-book of Dr. Borlase, and gives a good idea of an Urn in the inverted position so common in Cornwall. "The Urn," adds the MS. "is pecked round about the brim with some small indents made by the point of some tool, before the clay was hardened." Its shape was "inelegant" and the pottery "coarse."

DURVAL, or DERWELL.

DURVAL URN.
From a Drawing by Dr. Borlase.

Height .... 5 9/10 inches.
Width at bottom .... 3 inches.

MS. Drawings, p. 3. This Urn was found at Derwell, in the parish of Sancred, in 1753. "It is ornamented with indented fillets alternately dancette and horizontal. Its brim is a quarter-of-an-inch thick, the clay finer than any except that of the Kerris

Urn,[1] and somewhat ruddy, but neither so fine or red as that. The ashes well burnt; no sign of bones. Above it was found a flat cutt stone. It must have been a child's urn. It is in the keeping of Mr. Nicholas Cloke, at whose house I copied it, and at the same time was shewn an Antoninus of the large size: R. a soldier helmetted, sitting on the globe: Cos. III., brought him from the same parish."

Whereabouts on the Durval Downs this urn was found cannot now be determined. The summit of the hill which bears this name is surmounted by three barrows placed in a line, and about thirty paces apart. In one of these opened by the author in August, 1862, two long flat stones were found resting on their edge on the natural soil, and between them a great quantity of black incinerated earth, but no pottery or bones. In the second and middle one, a ring of stones had been placed round a granite rock, but this one, as well as the third, showed marks of previous disturbance.

On the south-eastern brow of the same hill are the traces of a large ring barrow, the area of which is strewn with heaps of small stones. It was originally forty-four feet in diameter, but only seven of the stones remain *in situ;* their height averages three feet.

---

[1] Figured at a subsequent page.

It may, therefore, be in any of these spots that this urn was found. On the south-western slope of the hill (viz., at Chigwidden), is a most remarkable fortified enclosure, in which, as will be seen at a future page, third brass Roman coins have been found.

The Durval Urn much resembles the drinking cups of the English Antiquaries; and as no bones were found in it, it is possible that a cinerary urn is yet undiscovered near the spot where it was disinterred, or *perhaps* an inhumated body.

TREWINARD.

Paroch. Mem. MS., page 14. "In the year 1750, March 1st, the workmen at Trewinard, (the seat of Christr. Hawkins, Esq.,) removing a barrow near the way coming from the west found an Earthen Urne. The workmen broke it to pieces before they saw what it was; perceiving marks of fire upon it, they took some of the earth inclosed and vanned it in water, thinking it to be tin, but, finding themselves disappointed, threw by the fragments of the Urne and the inclosed ashes. The Urne was placed on its mouth near the centre of the tumulus, which was mostly (and especially in the middle) of white spar stone. Round the urne was a little *septum* of stones set in order, open only at one end; on the top of the septum a broad flat stone, about two feet in diameter, which covered that and the urne. The bones in the urne were decayed and turned to clay."

FRAGMENTS OF THE URN FROM TREWINARD.
From a Drawing by Dr. Borlase.

From the fragments of this urn, here engraved, the vessel itself may be compared with that found at Angrowse, in Mullion, figured at a subsequent page. The portion with the handle, probably belongs, not to the upper rim, but to the same level on the vessel as the lower of the two horizontal lines figured on the other fragment.

KERRIS.

MS. Paroch. Mem., p. 6. "About 200 yards to the N.W. of Kerris House, (in the parish of Paul,) in the year 1723, some workmen removing an old hedge discovered a vault. It was about eight feet long, and six feet high, paved under foot with stone, and arched over with the same materials. Within, was a fair Urne of the finest red earth; it had no appearance of fire on it; it was found full of earth. The rim round the mouth is one inch deep." With it were found some brass coins now no more to be heard of. From the stress which Dr. Borlase lays, both here and in the *Antiquities of Cornwall*, p. 307, on the fairness and redness of this pottery, it seems not improbable that it was a piece of Samian ware; and a similar discovery at Chapel Euny, only a few miles off, renders this doubly probable. On this same estate of Kerris, stands a rude block of granite, nine feet broad and seven-and-three-quarters in height. By the side of this, the author made some excavations, but without any result. Two

THE KERRIS URN.
From a Drawing by Dr. Borlase.

Height .... 8¾ inches.
Diam. at mouth .... 5⅛ inches.
Ditto in swell ...... 6¾ inches.

hundred yards from this stone, and joining the lane leading into Kerris, are the remains of a remarkable oval enclosure, (a sketch of which is engraved by Borlase,) still called the Roundāgoe. It consists of a platform 150 feet long, by 107 broad, levelled on the summit of a gentle eminence. Two pillars, respectively 6 feet 6 inches and 7 feet in height, form part of a curious oblong recess mentioned and figured in the *Antiquities of Cornwall*, but of a " Kist-Vaen," six feet long by three-and-a-half feet wide, no trace can be found. There are no traces of hut circles within the enclosure, nor do the walls at any time seem to have been sufficiently lofty or substantial for purposes of defence; so that its origin and purpose must still remain, like that of the monument in the Deer-Park at Sligo,[1] (to which it bears some resemblance) a mystery still to be solved.

A second discovery was made on this same farm of Kerris, in the year 1844. At Kerris Vean, says Mr. Edmonds,[2] the author of the *Land's End District*, was opened a grave, eighteen feet long, four feet wide, and three feet deep, "containing fragments of urns, calcined human bones, charcoal, and a very rich black unctuous soil."

In this grave was also found a large fragment of

---

[1] Fergusson, *Rude Stone Monuments*, 234.
[2] *Report of the Penz. Nat. Hist. Society for* 1848.

a bowl of granite, "smoothly cut inside and outside." It would have been, judging from the fragment, four inches high, fourteen inches in diameter at the top,

KERRIS VAEN BOWL.
From a Drawing by Mr. Edmonds.

and eight at the bottom; and, when restored, its appearance would have been as given in the above sketch. The thickness of the vessel at top and bottom was one inch, but in the centre it increased to one-inch-and-three-quarters. The brim is marked by a small drill or trench running round it, and the lower part of the vessel was so rounded that it could not stand firmly on its base. In pl. xxv, of *Borlase's Antiquities*, a very similar bowl occurs, and both were probably corn-crushers.[1]

---

[1] This structure at Kerris would seem to be very similar to the Giant's Graves at Scilly, and also to that at Pennance. If so, it is possible that they also contained incinerated remains.

A grave, which from the description of the tenant farmer, appears to have resembled that at Kerris Vaen, was accidentally found a few years since, in the middle of the farm-yard at Castallack, in the same parish of Paul.

GOLDVADNEK.

The following is an extract from a MS. letter, in the possession of the author, from Thomas Tonkin, Esq. to Dr. Borlase, dated March 1st, 1727. "In 1700, a parcell of tinners, opening a burrow of stones in the parish of Gwendron, not far from Carnky, called Collbadnack Burrow, came at last to some large ones, disposed in the nature of a vault, in which they found an urn full of ashes, and a fine chequered brick pavement, (which, together with the urne, they ignorantly broke to pieces) with several Roman brass coins of the second size, and a small instrument of brass, set in ivory, which, I suppose, the Roman ladies made use of about their hair. The coins were much defaced. Two of them, with the instrument, were brought to me. On the first was very legible DIVA FAVSTINA. * * The other, as well as I could guess, was of Lucilla. * * * Since that, I had another given me of Marcus Antoninus Pius." This letter is inserted in the *Antiquities* at p. 308, where it is also stated that a first brass of Trajan, together with two second brass, one of Nerva, and one of Marcus Aurelius Antoninus were found at the same place.

KARNMENELEZ.

MS. Paroch. Mem. p. 43. "About half-a-mile to the east of Golvadnek Barrow is Karn-men-Elez, or the 'Karn stones of Angells.' It is a range or run of Karns, natural, intermixed with two large stone barrows bearing in a line nearly N. and S. In the southernmost Karn, I (*i.e.* Dr. Borlase) found many large flat stones, lying near one the other, like the coverings of cromlechs, having some rock basins on the top. These flat stones covered a narrow gutt about two feet wide and fifteen feet long. Near them lay many rude stone pillars from eight to ten feet long. About 200 yards to the North is a stone barrow very large; by the hollow in the middle, it has been searched, the stones being thrown up on every side. Here the man, who was my guide, told me that some coins of Julius Cæsar were found, which relation may probably have taken its rise from some Roman coins found here, (bearing the word Cæsar on them.) From this first barrow we kept on to the North about 200 paces, where we came to a natural Karn of flat rocks; the top rock was nineteen feet long by sixteen broad. Round it there was a ditch eight feet wide, edged with a mound of stones, rocks, and earth, which made a regular circle quite round the rock,[1] in the following manner.

About 200 yards more brought us to another barrow of stones. Searched this also had been, and in the middle of it a range of long stones in their natural order was enclosed and buried. On one side

KARNMENELEZ RING AND ROCK.
From a Drawing by Dr. Borlase.

of the barrow I perceived a stone wall, about seven feet high from the ground, which makes me think that the heap had formerly a more regular shape, and might have been built in the shape of a pyramid."

PERRAN SANDS.

The Urn here figured is copied from the drawing made by Borlase. There is, unfortunately, no de-

---

[1] This rock, in common with one at Trescow, Scilly, to which it bears a striking resemblance, was probably used for sepulchral purposes, *i.e.*, to burn the body upon.

scription of its discovery. It was of coarse clay, contained a large quantity of bones ill burnt, and was, it is believed, deposited at Pencarrow.

PERRAN URN.
From a Drawing by Dr. Borlase.

Height, (about) .... 11 inches.
Diam. at mouth .... 11 inches.
Do. at bottom................................ 5 inches.

ST. MARY'S, SCILLY.

Nat. Hist. of Cornwall, page 322, and plate. A plain urn, six-inches-and-a-half high, by seven-inches-and-a-quarter at its greatest diameter, and inclosing human bones, was found about the year 1754, in Mr. T. Smith's garden at Newport, on the island of St. Mary's. "It stood upon the natural clay, inclosed in a vault 4 feet 6 inches long, 2 feet 3 inches wide, and about 1 foot 3 inches deep. The sides of the vault were faced with stone; its covering, flat stones." Dr. Borlase mentions that he inserts it as the only one up to that time discovered in the islands, but several are said to have been found since.

KARN, MORVAH.

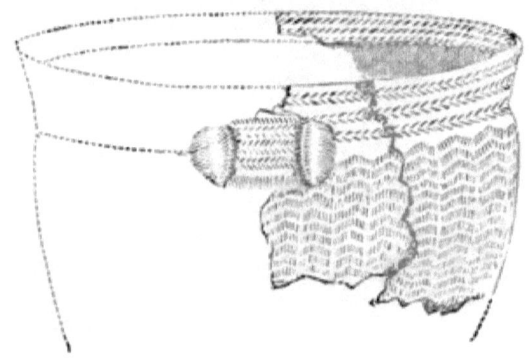

Fragment of Karn Urn.
From a Drawing by Dr. Borlase.

Height of fragment.................... 4½ inches.
Thickness........................ ⅜ths of an inch.

Nat. Hist., p. 322. The fragment here engraved was a portion of an urn found under a large heap of stones at Karn, in the parish of Morvah, in 1754. "The clay was fine and well burnt," "the *ansa* solid," and "the colour cinereous."

Like many other urns presently to be noticed, the wavy chevron pattern is, in this case, extended over the handle. On this same hill of Karn, on the side declining towards Morvah church, were formerly many small circles, supposed to be the ground-work of British huts.

The Rev. Malachi Hitchins, writing to the *Archæologia*, in 1802, mentions the fact that an urn with coins was found close to this place in the year 1789. "It was found," he says, "near the N.W. corner of a small enclosure, surrounded by a thick uncemented stone wall, at the foot of a very long and large stone inserted in the wall." It was about a foot from the surface, and covered by a flat stone of granite. No mention is made of any bones.

The Morvah Hill Barrow, where coins of Constantius have been found, is the next high ground to the East of Karn.

MISCELLANEOUS.

The following notices of sepulchral interments are from Hals, and Carte, and are quoted by Dr. Borlase.

1. "At Tencreek (in Creed parish) or Tencruck, *i.e.*, the fire bank or tumulus, is the sepulchre of one interred before the sixth century, whose body was burnt to ashes by fire, and his bones and ashes laid up in an urn, or earthen pot." Hals, MSS.
2. "In a barrow on Lamburn-downs, in the parish of Piran-san, was found an earthen pot, con-

taining about two gallons, wherein were lodged much ashes, some bones in small pieces, and charcoal; and by the side of the said pot were also found two small drinking cups of like clay, with several handles made of the same matter." Hals, MSS.

3. "On the open downs of Hundra, in this parish, (Piran-sands), are extant in a direct line extending from E. to W., twelve or fourteen notable barrows. * * * Some have been searched, and in the centre have been found 1, 2, 3, 4 or five large urns of clay, and in some of them ashes, charcoal, pieces of iron, and brass mony." Hals, MSS.

4. "The same author has recorded the discovery of a coin of the Emperor Gordian in a Cornish tumulus, but unfortunately does not name the locality.

5. Carte (vol. i, p. 103, *History of England*,) mentions that, "a little while before he came into Cornwall," (in the year 1714), "a fine Roman urn was discovered, with a cover to it, very large, on a hill opposite to Karnbré. It had ashes in it, and one coin of the bigness of a crown-piece, with an inscription on it very legible, shewing it to be a Medal of Augustus Cæsar." (?)

"Within less than ten years before I was

there," he continues, "a quantity of Roman coins was dug up in one of the barrows in the parish of Illogan. I have seen a great number of the coins found here in searching barrows, but none later than Lucilla and Faustina, found in those urns and barrows, but in other places down along to Valentinian the Third."

Carte also alludes to urns found at Ludgvan.

ST. AUSTELL, OR, GWALLON DOWNS.[1]

[*Philosophical Transactions*, 1740.] [MS. notes by Canon Rogers.]

The "One Barrow" on these Downs has been already described. Several others have been explored in the same vicinity; the first by Dr. Williams in the year 1740, with the following results:

"The body" of the barrow, according to that gentleman's account, "seemed to be composed of foreign, or adventitious earth. Near the centre we found a circular pit, one foot deep and the same diameter, dug out of the natural soil of the country, and two flat stones on it. The earth of this and the other barrows, of a yellowish colour, is known to be the natural soil of a hill a mile distant from them." "It deserves our serious observation, that the stones

---

[1] The barrows on these downs number in all about twenty. They run in straight lines of from three to seven.

Near them, is a "Menhir" or Long-stone, mentioned in Davies Gilbert's *Cornwall*, vol. i, p. 193.

which compose the heap over the cylindrical pit, were brought from places both high and low situated, and many miles distant from one another, as the Par, Polmeor Cliff, Hainsbarrow, Pentuan and Carnclays."

"Near the outward edge of one of these barrows an urn was discovered under two flat stones. It is composed of burnt or calcined earth, very hard and very black inside. In it were seven quarts of burnt ashes; the urn will hold two gallons or more." The height was thirteen-and-a-half inches; the diameter at mouth, eight inches; at the middle, eleven inches; and at the bottom, six-inches-and-a-half.

It is probable that the fragments of this same urn afterwards became the property of a gentleman of the neighbourhood, well versed in antiquarian lore, the Rev. Richard Hennah. If so, they are now to be found in the Truro Museum, accompanied by the following note:—"Found in a barrow on St. Austell Down, filled with human ashes, about 1740 or 1750. It (the urn) had four small handles, and is described in the Archæologia. It was given to me by the late Mr. Hennah, who had it from his uncle, Oct. 1818. J. Mayers."

Mr. Davies Gilbert, vol. ii, p. 869, mentions that, on the 29th of May, 1805, Mr. Hennah opened a barrow on the same Downs, which was found to contain a sepulchral urn.

The fragments of this urn were presented by the late Rev. Canon Rogers, to the Truro Museum, he

POTTERY FROM ST. AUSTELL DOWNS.
From a Drawing by Canon Rogers.

having received them from Mr. Hennah. The following are the measurements of the vessel. Internal diameter at mouth five-and-a-quarter inches; ditto at middle ten inches. Thickness from three-eighths to half-of-an-inch. Height (probably) ten to twelve inches. It contained five quarts of human bones.

An attempted restoration of the Urn will be found in Mr. Gilbert's work, and also in the MSS. of Canon Rogers, kindly lent to the author by J. J. Rogers, Esq., of Penrose. It is from the latter of these that the above engraving of the fragments is taken.

In the note accompanying these MSS., it is said

that this urn was found, not in a separate barrow but in the outer edge of the "One Barrow" previously noticed. This, however, can hardly be the case, as the One Barrow seems to have been cleared away for agricultural purposes four years previously. It is much to be regretted that the records of the explorations of these barrows have been so greatly confused together and mislaid, and that the pottery, having passed through so many hands, has not been properly labelled. Several fragments of other urns, probably found in the same vicinity, and deposited at Truro by Canon Rogers and Mr. Mayers, have thus been rendered completely valueless.[1]

PELYNT.

[*Bond's East and West Looe.*] [*Accounts of Barrows in the Parish of Pelynt*, by Jno. Couch, Esq., ditto by W. H. Box, Esq., printed in the *Journal of the Roy. Institution of Cornwall.*]

In a field, a quarter of a mile south of Pelynt

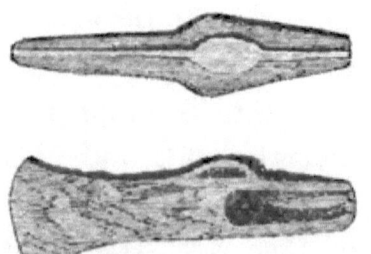

CELT FROM A BARROW NEAR ST. AUSTELL.

[1] Among the MSS. of the late Canon Rogers is the above drawing of a bronze celt "found *in a barrow* in making the road from St. Austell to Charlestown. A.D. 1791."

Church, and half-a-mile distant from the encampment known as Berry Rings, are ten Barrows, varying from two to five feet in height. Ever since Mr. Bond wrote his account of East and West Looe, (in 1823), this field has been known as a spot most fruitful in Antiquities. "In the highway," he says, "just at the bottom of the said field, a few years since, a grave was discovered by some men mending the highway. It was formed by four stones on their edges, and a covering stone. In this Kist-Vaen was an urn, with burnt ashes in it; and round the urn were piled, in a regular manner, the unburnt (?) remains of human bones. I went to Pelynt purposely to see this curiosity, but found the grave had been filled up and its contents buried. The urn was described to me by a man who saw it as having ornaments of flowers and leaves on its outside, and that it fell into sheards when touched."

Jonathan Couch, of Polperro, Esq., F.L.S., writing in 1845, mentions, that several years previously, in cutting through one of the barrows in the "Five Barrow" field, as it was called, "the only ancient object brought to light was a celt, formed of a compound metal with much the appearance of copper, and much resembling those engraved by Borlase."[1]

---

[1] This celt was in the possession of Mr. Box, of East Looe. Where it is now the author cannot ascertain. A rough drawing of it is in the Truro Museum, from which it seems much like the Godolphin one. See page 41.

"About the end of the year 1834," continues Mr. Couch, "while ploughing in this field the ploughshare came in contact with a stone in one of the smaller barrows, and removed it; when the workmen observed beneath the stone several small fragments of bone, mixed with pieces of charcoal; but there was no urn nor the fragments of one. Near them, but not in the cavity with the bones, was a metallic instrument."

This instrument, now deposited in the Truro Museum, is of precisely the same description as that found at Angrowse, in Mullion, figured at a subsequent page. Its present length is three-and-three-quarter inches, but it was probably several inches longer. Like the Angrowse specimen, and also like one found at Benallack, near Par, this dagger was fastened to the half by rivets, two of which are still in their places. It is of bronze, and on cutting it, shines like brass.

The farmer next proceeded to cart away for manure the largest barrow, nearest to the south hedge; "but after uncovering to the depth of nearly three feet, he found that he had laid bare a huge bed of stones," and desisted from his work.

The subsequent operations were conducted under Mr. Couch's inspection. "I found," he says, "that the body of the mound consisted of the small ordinary stones of the country, unmixed with earth, and thrown together without order; but the surface of these stones, or the outer layer, was formed of a regular arrangement of flat, and much larger stones, rough and uncut, but fitted to lie smooth, and serve as a covering to the others. In the middle of this heap, level with the surface of the natural ground, and not enclosed in any limited space, there was a considerable quantity of black ashes, which had been evidently burnt on the spot. There was no urn; and the only work of art that was found, was a hammer formed of stone, pronounced by competent mineralogists to be greenstone, a kind not found in a natural condition within a considerable distance."

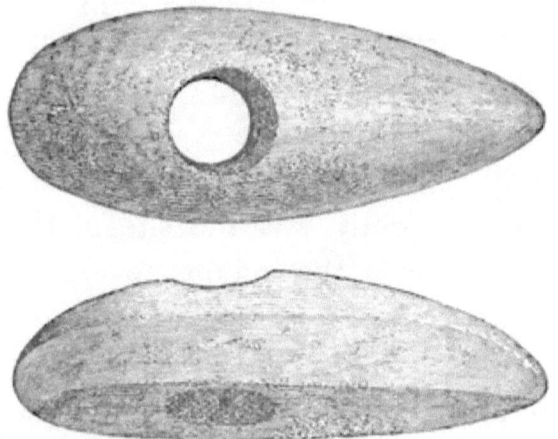

STONE HAMMER IN THE TRURO MUSEUM.
From a Drawing by John Evans, Esq., F.R.S., (copied by his permission).
Length.......................... 5 inches.

The weight is ten-and-three-quarter ounces, and

the shape is so remarkable that the author is induced to present an engraving of it in this place.¹

From the above date, until November, 1845, these barrows remained unnoticed, when the public interest was again directed to them by the labours of Messrs. Cook, McLauchlan and W. H. Box.²

"On the 24th of November, 1845, a party of labourers were directed to cut a trench, nine-and-a-half feet wide, through the centre of the largest barrow, which is eighty feet in diameter, in a line extending from east to west. About three feet from the western end, and two below the surface, the workmen arrived at a black greasy mould mixed with particles of charcoal, which occupied the entire breadth of the trench, and extended to within a foot of its centre. Beneath this, to a depth varying from two to five inches, was a bed of incinerated brown-coloured clay, having much the appearance of coarse brick. This evidently was the site of the funeral pile. On arriving at the middle, several fragments of an urn were found intermixed with portions of bones, and dark earth; but no stones were seen that could have protected the remains from the surrounding soil. The urn, from the parts collected, appeared, both in manufacture and material, to have been of

---

[1] "I have never," says Mr. Evans, "seen any other Stone-hammer of this form found in Britain, nor can I call to mind any such in continental museums."—*Ancient Stone Implements.*

[2] See *Journal of the Royal Institution of Cornwall for* 1846, page 43.

the rudest description. On completing the trench, it was observed that each of its sides was marked by strata of different colours, extending horizontally over ten or twelve feet of its centre. The uppermost was a stiff black loam, varying in depth from three to four inches, with large pieces of charcoal imbedded in it; this was separated by a layer of common earth, from another of similar dimensions and texture, of a deep orange colour, which, like the former, rested on a vein of earth. Supporting these was a third, about two inches in depth, that from its light grey appearance, was at first thought to be sand, but on examination, was found to possess more of the character of clay than either of the former. The space beneath to the floor of the barrow, which was eighteen or twenty inches, was occupied by a bed of the natural soil. The origin of these coloured veins must ever remain a subject for conjecture. Their uniform extent and regularity afford strong evidences of design in their arrangement, and, as the surrounding neighbourhood furnishes no soils like them, either in colour or conformation, we cannot easily imagine them to be composed of primitive strata.

"The examination of the other barrows was conducted in the same way as the first. The highest was scarcely three feet above the level of the field, and the walls of the trenches in each were marked by the light grey vein, which it will be recollected was the lowest of the series already described. A thin belt of the deep orange was also seen in one, crowning its most elevated point, to the extent of about three or four feet; hence it may be inferred that a similar arrangement of these coloured veins characterised the whole, and that the more superficial had been destroyed by the plough.

"The sites of the pyres in all, both in extent and appearances, were alike, and were situated west of their centres.

"The barrow next examined, was situated due west of the first, distant about sixty-five paces; its greatest elevation was about three feet, and its diameter sixty. On arriving at the middle, the workmen, a little below the surface, discovered a flint celt (of which a sketch is here given), and a few inches beneath it, a large stone, which proved to be the covering slab of a Kist-Vaen, or stone coffin."

FLINT CELT AND "THUMB-FLINT," PELYNT.

This celt is three-inches-and-a-half in length, by

one-and-a-half in breadth, flat on one side, and rounded on the other; it displays evident marks of secondary chipping.

The Kist, now placed in the Truro Museum, measures two feet in length, by one foot in breadth, and is 1 foot 2 inches deep. "The ends were pointed east and west, and the whole structure was composed of twelve stones. Seven stones formed the actual chest, four of which were fixed in the ground on their edges, and constituted the sides and ends. The side stones described the brim, which was irregular, by the south one being from one-and-a-half to two inches higher than that on the north. The ends were shorter and supported two quartzose blocks, which, by resting their extreme angles on the ends of the side uprights, projected from three to four inches over the cavity within. The bottom stone accurately filled the area formed by the frame work of the chest, but was cracked longitudinally through its centre, and slightly elevated along the course of the fracture. The cover was composed of five stones, ingeniously arranged for the purpose of protection; two, almost square, were placed across the chest and rested on the sides, supporting two others which were long and narrow, and placed lengthways. The partition lines of these were so small that no soil could penetrate them; and from their crossing each other at right angles, additional protection was obtained, while the crowning slab which overlapped the whole completed the cover, and insured perfect security." The contents of the kist were a quantity of delicately white fragments of calcined bones, the greater part situated at the eastern end; they were the remains of one person only. Not a particle of charcoal or ashes could be detected among the fragments of bone. A bed of coarse gravel beneath the flooring stone of the kist led to the supposition that a spring of water took its rise in that spot.

"The third and last barrow examined, was situated about sixteen paces south-west of the second. The centre was occupied by a considerable number of large stones. Nothing of interest was discovered on their removal. Towards the west end, and a little above the floor of the barrow, a small flint (figured with the larger one above), was found, which nearly resembled in size and figure a common gunflint. The bed of the pyre was thickly strewn with fragments of charcoal, some of which were large and evidently derived from the oak."

The author has given almost *in extenso* the account of the opening of these tumuli, because he believes that in no other instance will so many minor yet interesting details be found to have been so carefully collected, and circumstantially recorded, as in this instance they have been by Mr. Box.

NEWQUAY.

[From the *Journal of Royal Institution of Cornwall.* 1840, p. 60.]

Canon Rogers has preserved an account of a barrow opened by him on the 21st of May, 1840, near the town of Newquay.

The Barrow was situated in an elevated situation near the cliff, about a mile from the town. It was twelve feet in height, surrounded by a trench about five feet wide and nearly the same deep, cut in part through the slate rock.[1] Much of the mound had been carried away for manure, and, during its removal, urns were found but not preserved.

The excavation was commenced at the base of the barrow, and marks of fire were soon perceived, burnt earth being intermixed with yellowish clay. Nothing was discovered but "a few broken flints."

A trench was next commenced through the centre of the tumulus. The work was at first easy, owing to the soft nature of the earth which composed it; but as it proceeded, a layer of quarry rubbish had to be cut through, and finally a heap of large stones, quartz, lime-stone, and slate, piled irregularly on each other,

---

[1] It is one of the peculiarities of the ditches enclosing the cliff castles in this neighbourhood, that they are excavated in the slate. This is particularly noticeable at Trevalga, and Bedruthan Castles.

was laid bare. Most of the stones bore evident marks of fire; the top of the pile was about six feet below the summit of the barrow. At the bottom were flat stones, the under sides of which were very black from the effect of fire. Nothing, however, was found beneath this pile. "But, though disappointed," (says the Canon), "with regard to the principal place of sepulture, in the progress of our excavation, I observed what appeared to be the side of an Urn of rude pottery, resting diagonally with its mouth downwards on a stone, and a stone placed above it. The Urn was so much decayed that we could only take it out in fragments. It was filled with human bones, which, at first, appeared as white as snow. The Urn is of coarse pottery, very rudely ornamented." As far as could be judged from the remains, it seems to have resembled the Urn found in Piran San.

The fragments of this Urn are now in the Truro Museum. It is not ornamented with the chevron pattern, but has small indentations on the rim, similar to that from Penquite, engraved at page 144.

There is, in the same collection, another Urn, also in a fragmentary state, found in the same vicinity, namely, on the top of the cliff[1] between Newquay

---

[1] The author has recently been informed, that a remarkable *long* grave was found under another tumulus, also situated on this cliff. It is said to have contained human remains, and to have been divided into two chambers, a long and a short one.

and Lower St. Columb Porth. This vessel, for which the Institution is indebted to the Rev. C. Painter, is of extremely coarse pottery, badly baked, and seems to have been very similar in shape to the one found by Canon Rogers.

GLEN-DORGAL.

[From a communication to the Royal Institution of Cornwall, by F. Rodd, Esq., 1850.]

GLEN-DORGAL URN.
From a Photograph by Mr. Argall, of Truro.

Height .... 13 inches.
Diam. at mouth .... 9 inches.

The beautiful villa called Glen-Dorgal, the summer residence of Francis Rodd, Esq., of Trebartha, is situated on the western or rather southern side of the little cove, called Lower St. Columb Porth, near which the last-mentioned Urn was discovered. Close to the house, the above Urn was found. The barrow from which it was taken was situated on a rocky eminence, opposite Porth Island. On removing a flat stone, scarcely, if at all, underneath the natural surface of the ground, "the Urn was found, in an inverted position, in a pit about two feet deep, excavated between the fragments of the rock." The mouth of the pit was surrounded by four flat stones, upon which rested the cover. "On raising the Urn a quantity of human bones with black earth and ashes fell out into the pit. The whole had evidently undergone the action of fire."

This urn, as will be observed, has two fine handles, resembling those on the Tresvenneck vessel. The rude diagonal lines, "carelessly scratched with a tool round the upper part," present certainly the rudest, and possibly the earliest example of the chevron pattern, found on any Cornish Urn.

TREVELGUE CLIFF CASTLE.

The line of coast of which Trevelgue forms a centre, and which may be roughly included in the name Watergate Bay (*i.e.*, from Towan Head to

Park Head) is completely studded with objects of interest to the Antiquary. There is not a headland or high portion of the cliff which is not crowned by tumuli or entrenchments, sometimes indeed by both.[1] Immediately opposite the spot where the Glen-Dorgal Urn was found, is the fortified island of Trevalga or Trevelgue,[2] separated from the shore by a narrow fissure in the rock, and strongly guarded against the land side by six distinct lines of earthwork. Within these entrenchments, and perched on the very summit of the rocky island, stands a barrow, of the 'bowl,' or rather 'bell' shape.

A pit sunk from the surface to the base of this barrow in July, 1872, proved, that like others in the same neighbourhood, the mound consisted of a covering of earth enclosing a 'cairn' of stones. Among the latter, several showed signs of fire. No interment was discovered, but the author hopes on some future occasion to make a fair trial of the whole mound, by driving a trench across it.

Perhaps the most remarkable feature in this cliff castle is the great quantity of flint-chips which may be picked up among the débris of the walls, and on the point of the Island. Several of these (one of

---

[1] Tumuli frequently occur in Cornwall within the area of hill or cliff castles, as at Castle-an-dinas, near St. Columb, &c.

[2] For a description of two other large tumuli on the higher part of this estate, see page 81, *et seq.*

them in form like a small hatchet) are preserved in the Truro Museum.[1]

A low tumulus, opened by the author, on the land side of the fortification contained a burnt interment, placed in a small cup-shaped hollow, scooped in the natural soil.

PLACE, near FOWEY.

[From a paper by J. T. Treffry, Esq., in the *Journal of the Royal Institution of Cornwall*, read Nov. 6th, 1840.]

THE PLACE URN.
From a Photograph by Mr. Argall.

Height .... 8 inches.
Diam. at mouth .... 6 inches.

---

[1] These flints were not found in a barrow, and have, therefore, been incorrectly labelled in the Museum.

In the early part of October, 1840, some workmen were employed in making a new road into the town of Fowey, to avoid the steep hill leading to that place from the west. Just under the brow of the hill, and 215 feet south of the old road, they struck on a large stone, placed horizontally. This stone was three feet from the surface, but immediately under the field mould, which, in this place, was rich, deep, and of a dark colour. Under the stone was a square pit, fourteen inches deep, on the bottom of which, the urn, here engraved, rested, at a depth of 4 feet 5 inches from the surface. The sides of the pit were fenced with four square slate stones. The Urn contained human ashes. The pottery is of a yellowish colour, the baking having been externally so slight as not to change the natural colour of the clay. The pattern imprinted round the vessel might have been made by a common stick from the hedge.

By the kindness of Mr. Treffry, the Urn has been deposited in the Museum at Truro.

GERRANS.

[From a paper by Dr. Winn, in the *Journal of the Royal Institution of Cornwall*, for 1844.]

This exceedingly handsome and characteristic Urn was found at Merrows, in Gerrans, on the 4th of

May, 1844. Not far from where it was discovered, towards the east, lies the Veryan Beacon, opened by

THE GERRANS URN.
From a Photograph by Mr. Argall.

Height .... 13⅜ inches.
Diam. at mouth .... 9 inches.

Mr. Adams, and previously noticed at page 155: while a quarter of a mile to the south may be seen the remains of the so-called Castle of King Gerennius. In this neighbourhood too was found the curious Portscatha Urn, drawings of the fragments of which will be found at page 206. "The spot whence the Urn was removed" say Dr. Winn, "is situated in a field about fifty yards from the junction of two gentle-sloping hills, and a quarter of a mile from the sea." There seems to have been no indication of a barrow, as the farmer in ploughing, struck his plough-share against the stone which covered the Urn. It stood in an upright position, between three and four feet from the surface, covered by two slate stones. It was filled with calcined bones, which were identified as those of a full-grown person, and ashes were found round the outside of the bottom of the vessel. The clay is fairly baked, and the pottery is of a slightly ruddy hue. The chevron pattern, between six horizontal lines, is neatly executed, and bears evidence of having been formed by the application of twisted cords, or a grass rope, while the clay was wet. The four handles, as will be seen presently, are by no means infrequent on Cornish pottery.

PORTSCATHA.

Within a short distance of the spot where the Gerrans Urn was found, is the cove of Portscatha. Near this place, in removing an old Barrow, the fragments of an Urn were found, and kindly forwarded by Mr. Russell to the Penzance Museum, in 1868. Further than this, no details of the occurrence have been recorded. The fragments are, however, so remarkable, that two of them are here engraved. From these, it appears that the vessel was cylindrical, of large proportions, and formed of very fine yellow clay. Although it is highly improbable that any Cornish Urns were sun-baked, this one certainly has the appearance of being so, as the pottery is excessively hard, though the clay has

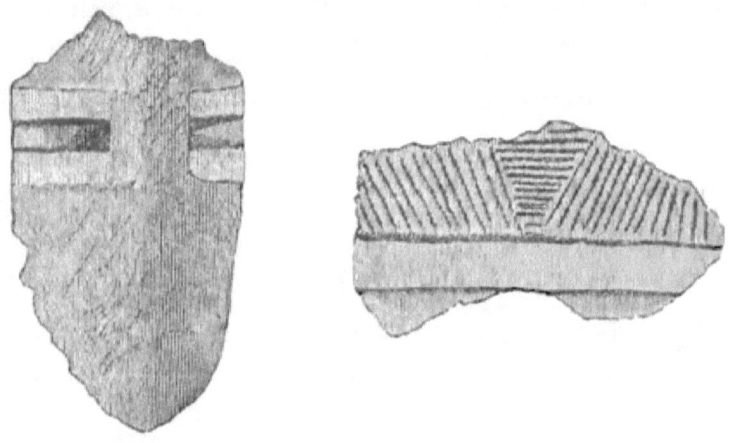

Fig 1. Fig 2.
POTTERY FROM THE PORTSCATHA URN.

never lost its original colour or appearance. It is ornamented by two bands, or ridges, in high relief, each seven-eighths-of-an-inch in width, running round the vessel, formed apparently by the tightening of bands while the clay was wet. The trench formed between these ridges was spanned in two, if not in more places, by bridges of clay forming cleats or handles through which a cord might have been passed. (See fig. 1.) The upper part of the vessel was ornamented with diagonal and horizontal lines, as in figure 2. Altogether this specimen is unique among the Cornish sepulchral pottery.

TREVELLO KARN.

THE TREVELLO URNS.

LARGER URN.   SMALLER URN.
From a Photograph by Mr. Preston.

Height ...... 1 foot and ⅝ of an inch.   Height .... 5 and 3-10ths inches.
Diam. at mouth .... 9 inches.   Diam. at mouth, 3 and 4-5ths inches.

Trevello Karn is a romantic pile of granite rocks, forming an abrupt wall to the bleak moors which occupy a portion of the parish of Paul. In the year 1839, during the removal of a barrow of stones immediately above this Karn, a circular piece of walling, four feet high, was discovered. It was formed of large stones, set on their edges, and within the enclosure were the two Urns, figured above. They were placed with their mouths downwards; the smaller one resting on a concavity in a square stone; the larger one, in a hollow scooped out of the natural ground. The large Urn inclosed bones, partly calcined; the small one was half filled with fine dust. The former is the most symmetrically formed, as well as the most characteristic example of the cylindrical type of Urn; while the latter is evidently intended to be a miniature representation of its larger companion. Although the Trevello Urn is not so well baked as that from Gerrans, yet the similarity in design between the two is unmistakeable, and goes far to prove, that this particular type of vessel was not merely the freak of a local potter, but that it extended over the entire district to which these pages relate.

The Penzance Museum is indebted to John Millett, of Bosaverne, Esq., for these interesting Urns, now preserved in their collection.

TRANNACK.

[From the *Report of the Penzance Nat. Hist. Society* for 1848.]

The author is entirely indebted to the labours of Mr. Edmonds, author of the *Land's End District*, for the account of two Urns, found (the one enclosed in the other) at Trannack, in the parish of Madron, in the year 1824. Some labourers, employed by Mr. Pengelly, the proprietor of the estate, were engaged in levelling a tumulus, nine feet in diameter. On arriving at a depth of five feet from the surface, they came to the "natural floor," on which rested five or six Urns. The largest of

THE TRANNACK URNS.
From a Photograph by Mr. Preston.

Height of inner one .... 8⅞ inches.
Diam. at mouth .... 7¾ inches.

these was thirteen inches high, and nine inches in diameter; two others, (those here engraved) were smaller, and a remarkable fact about them was, that the one was encased in the other. Whether the unadorned Urn was a subsequent interment to that with the chevron pattern, which surrounded it, or whether the inner one was considered not sufficiently substantial, and required protection, cannot now be determined. Both these vessels contained calcined bones, but what was discovered in the others is not mentioned. "From beneath the same tumulus was taken a smoothly-rounded piece of granite, whose greatest diameter was four-and-a-quarter inches, and its least three-and-a-quarter, through the middle of which was a small hole; the thickness in the centre was one-and-a-quarter inch, diminishing gradually towards the circumference."

CONQUER DOWNS.

URN FROM CONQUER DOWNS.
From a Photograph by Mr. Preston.

Height .... 1 foot.
Diam .... 7 and 9-10ths inches.

The Barrow in which this Urn was found was forty-five feet in diameter, and six feet high. A section of it will be be found in the *Gentleman's Magazine* for 1865, from the pencil of Mr. Blight. From this, it appears that it was a stone cairn encircled by a ring of large stones. The Urn was discovered by some labourers, who accidentally cut through the barrow. It was standing in the centre, mouth downwards on the flat stone. "No regular Kist-Vaen had been formed, but the stones were carefully built around the Urn, which was protected above by a large slab." The vessel contained burnt bones, the action of fire being evident on the surrounding stones. The Urn is remarkable for its shape, which is that of a perfect cylinder. The pottery is of a greyish colour, very indifferently baked, and the ornamentation represents a rude type of the chevron and indented pattern. For this relic, the Penzance Museum is indebted to the Hon. Mrs. Gilbert, on whose estate it was found. In consequence of the discovery of this vessel, another stone cairn ninety-four yards north-west was soon after explored, but it had probably been rifled before; nothing being found, but a broken flint pebble, and the bones of an animal.

The name of the Downs, where these barrows are situated, is remarkable, especially as they are bounded to the south by the circular entrenchments, known as Castle-an-dinas,[1] and would afford a most admirable stand-point for an army defending the Western or Land's End district.

---

[1] "Conquer" may possibly be only a corruption of "Carn-caer," signifying the "hill castle."

BRANE COMMON, SANCRED.

In the year 1842, about 200 yards north of the Cave and Hut Circles at Chapel Euny, two Urns were found by some labourers while pulling down a hedge. One of them broke in pieces; but the other was conveyed to the Rev. Mr. Buller, then Vicar of St. Just, who presented it to the Penzance Museum. The vessel is of the vase-shaped variety, and has two rough unpierced bosses or handles. The clay retains its original colour, although it seems sufficiently baked. From the labourer who found these Urns the following particulars were obtained. They were filled with ashes and bones, and by the side of each lay a neatly formed oblong stone, perforated at one end. He also remembered that a "*knife*" had been found, but carried away and lost by another workman. The present height of the Urn is one foot, and the diameter at the mouth eight-and-three-quarter inches. In form it much resembles the ruder Angrowse Urn figured at a subsequent page.

Of the two perforated stones, the larger measures three-and-a-half inches in length, and is formed of a black marble; while the smaller one, a brown sandstone, (though not quite so long), is double the thick-

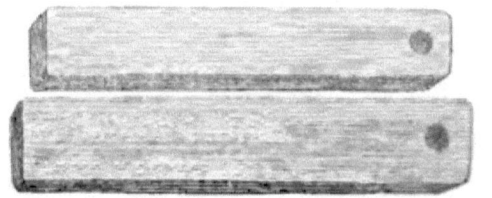

TWO PERFORATED STONES, FROM BRANE COMMON.

ness, namely two-fifths-of-an-inch.[1] They would seem to belong to the same class of relics as the spindle whorls, so often picked up in or near the hut circles. Caer Bran, a circular hill-castle, lies about a quarter of a mile east of the spot where these Urns were found.

BOLEIT, IN ST. BURYAN.

The two groups of tumuli, next to be noticed, those at Boleit and Boscawen-ûn, both in the same parish, and at a distance of only two miles apart as the crow flies, acquire a special interest, from their proximity to circles of upright stones, and from the evidence which their contents may therefore be ex-

---

[1] Implements of stone or bone, pierced at *both* ends, are not uncommon. See *Ancient Stone Implements*, by John Evans, F.R.S., p. 382.

pected to throw on the age of those monuments of which they seem to form a part.[1]

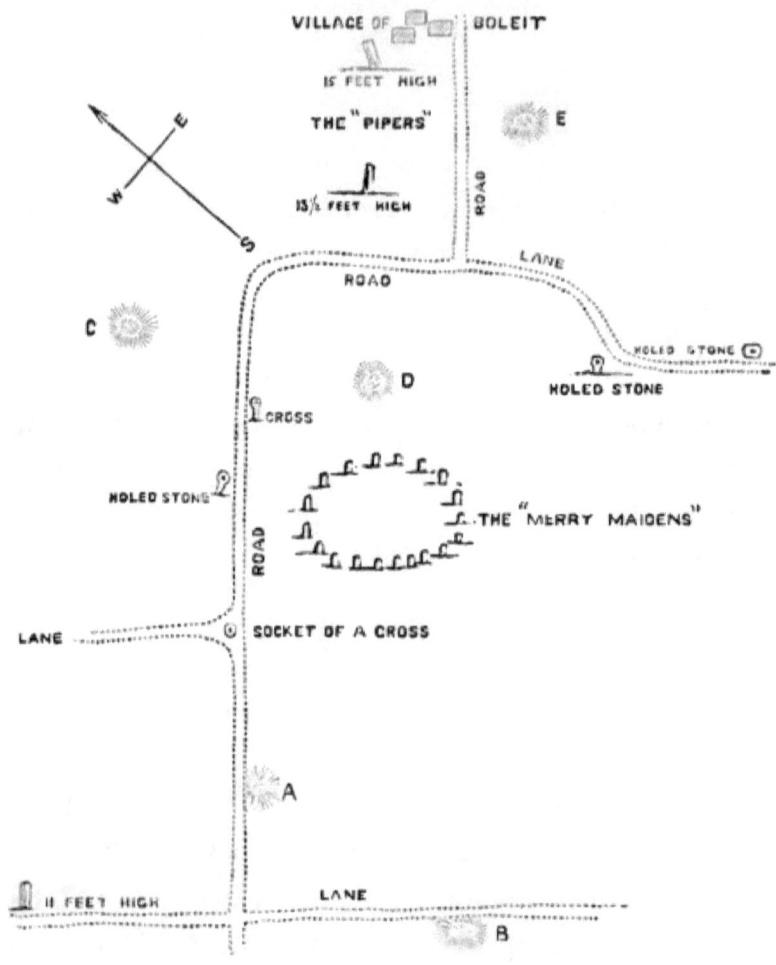

PLAN OF MEGALITHIC REMAINS AT ROSEMODDRESS AND BOLEIT.

Some idea of the manner in which the Boleit, and

---

[1] See 'Addenda B, for a barrow near another of these circles, at Boskednan.'

Rosemoddress, megalithic remains are grouped together may be derived from the accompanying plan. Before proceeding to notice the contents of the barrows, it may be as well to remark that at this place there are most distinct traditions of *a battle*.[1] The author, recently, spent several days in examining the ground, and collecting these traditions. An old man informed him that the soldiers who died in the great fight, (which lasted several days), were buried in a long trench (not included in the plan) on the slope of a hill to the eastward of the village, but that when this trench was dug over a few years since, no bones were found. Another story related that a vault immediately beneath the farm yard at Boleit contained the bodies of the slain, but "when this shall be discovered," added the old man, "'tis said that day will be the Judgment."[2] The "Pipers", by the same tradition, represent the positions of the chieftains in front of their respective armies; and a "wise man," reported to be living in "Buryan church-town," has it *on record*, that their names were *Howel* and *Athelstane*.[3] In confirmation of the story of the battle,

---

[1] Had Dr. Fergusson visited this Cornish "battle field," he might have still further elaborated his theory. The above was written before the appearance of his *Rude Stone Monuments*.

[2] The inhabitants were in consequence rather timid, when the author proposed to dig in search of the place.

[3] It has been previously mentioned, that on searching the ground around these pillars, no sepulchral remains were found.

the word Boleit, pronounced Bollay, has been said to signify the "House of the slaughter," from Bo or Bod, "a house" or "a grave," and Ladh, "a killing." Bo-lait, "a milk house" looks perhaps a more likely derivation; but the name Goon Rith which designates the land to the west of the circle, and where a third great stone is placed, is, undoubtedly, the "Red Downs," a name which, as there is no appearance of that colour in the soil, looks strangely as if they had once been "bathed in blood." By the side of this stone was found a sand-stone pebble, flattened on one side and evidently used as a whetstone. No tradition attaches to the three Holed Stones. The circle, which gives to the estate the name Rosemoddress, or "Ring Down," is composed of nineteen stones, and measures seventy-five feet in diameter. It is remarkable for the equality in height and appearance of the granite stones which compose it, their inner faces being almost invariably smooth and regular.

Of the barrows which surround it, one (A in the plan) has been already described at page 107. It contained a fallen longstone, and a Kist-Vaen, under which, it will be remembered, was found a large quantity of burnt bones. The barrow marked B has been so much injured by the formation of the road which passes through it, as to leave no hope of any further discovery in that quarter. In the Barrow, marked C, an Urn was found before Dr. Borlase[1] wrote his MS. notes, and was forwarded to the then Lord Falmouth. At D, in a line with the "Pipers" and the circle, but much nearer the latter, stood a barrow, now entirely removed, in which a workman named Eddy, not many years since, came upon an Urn, which he immediately broke in pieces. The only one of these barrows of the opening of which we have any details is that at E. In this, in the year 1847, was found an Urn, described by Mr. Edmonds, as being twenty inches high, and sixteen wide. The Kist-Vaen in which it was placed, was "surrounded by *two* circular walls, four feet high, the one about ten, the other eighteen feet in diameter, each consisting of a row of unshapen stones laid on their edges." The mouth of the urn was upwards, and it contained a considerable quantity of ashes. A cairn of stones had been heaped over the whole.

Mr. Edmonds has given a very correct drawing of the perforated cleat, or handle, of this vessel, but the resemblance between it and that found at Angrowse in Mullion, and figured at a subsequent page, is so great that the same engraving will here serve for them both. The fashion of the vessel, as well as the pattern and pottery, seems to have been very similar, and is another reason to believe that these peculiar

---

[1] See his MS. *Parochial Memoranda*.

types were not formed from the design of a merely local potter. Amongst the materials brought together to form the cairn, "were two beautifully rounded mullars, quite perfect, and smoothly flattened on the under surfaces." The smaller one is five inches high, and seven-and-a-half in its greatest diameter. There was also found in the cairn a flat stone two feet square, having in one of its surfaces a very smooth concavity, one foot in diameter, and two or three inches deep. Into this mill the mullar fitted exactly.[1]

Besides these discoveries, both Hals and Borlase mention the fact, that numerous urns were in their day taken up in and around Bolcit. On the slope of the hill to the east of the village, pottery is still found in great abundance, mixed with ashes and burnt wood. About a quarter of a mile to the north-east is the subterranean structure known as the "Fogou." Altogether, the tradition of a battle field seems to be borne out to a striking extent by the evidences of mortality, which, in all directions, are strewn over the ground.

BOSCAWEN ÛN.[2]

As in the case of Rosemoddress Circle, so in

---

[1] These implements are precisely similar to those so often found on the sites of the 'British Huts.'

[2] Camden mentions Boscawen-ûn in the following terms: "Not far from

that of Boscawen-ûn, several tumuli are to be seen in its immediate vicinity. In the autumn of 1864, two of these were explored. The first is situated about thirty yards south-east of the circle. It was composed chiefly of earth, and was from six to seven feet high. Through the centre a broad trench was cut, during which operation ashes were frequently met with. When near the middle, a flat stone was discovered, under which was a pit hollowed out in the hard clay soil. In this, were found ashes, minute chips of calcined bones, and one or two nodules of bronze, probably the rivets of a dagger. Two other pits occurred further on; in one of which, a few more ashes and bones were found.

The plan on the next page represents the second barrow, which was explored on the same day. Its construction is highly interesting, and throws a considerable light on the subject of urn burial, and "ring barrows" in general. A circle of stones, on edge, surrounds a large granite rock, twelve feet by eleven, and 2 feet 10 inches thick. This rock is natural, and was never moved. Its upper face is smooth, and in it has

---

hence, in a place call'd Biscaw-woune, are nineteen stones set in a circle, about 12 foot distant one from another; and in the center, there stands one much larger than any of the rest. One may probably conjecture this to have been some trophy of the Romans, under the later Emperors; or of Athelstane, the Saxon, after he had subdued Cornwall." A common-sense view of the case, before antiquaries saw any necessity for a Bronze Age. The tradition of Athelstane's coming to Cornwall, although unauthorised by history, is very common in the country.

been sunk a cavity, (A) 1 foot 6 inches long, by 1 foot 1 inch broad. "This upper part of the rock," observes Mr. Blight, "appears originally to have been exposed

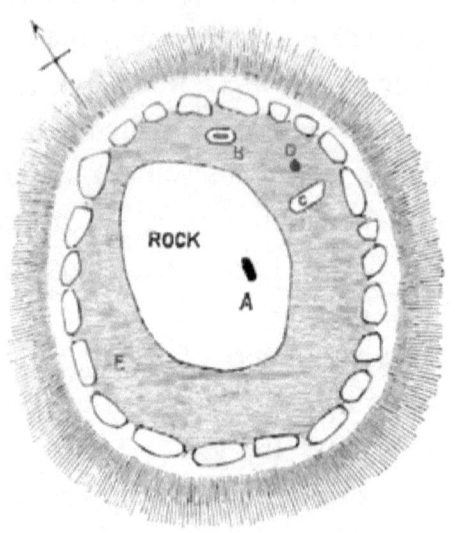

PLAN OF BOSCAWEN-ÛN RING-BARROW.
From a Drawing by J. T. Blight, Esq., F.S.A.

to view, though it had become overgrown by vegetation, and formed the summit of the barrow." In digging round this central stone, between it and the encircling ring, at the depth of about two feet, was found the block of granite, (B) figured at page 221. It was eighteen inches in length by twelve inches in breadth, and nine inches thick. In its surface was a concavity, four inches deep, artificially scooped out: and, like that found at Boleit, it is precisely the same description of mill which is always cropping up on the sites of ancient British hut-villages in the neighbourhood. As it had been broken, it was useless as a mill, and was therefore thrown in among the other stones to form the cairn. As Mr. Blight observes, its original purpose was "for bruising or grinding grain." A few feet further on was a stone marked

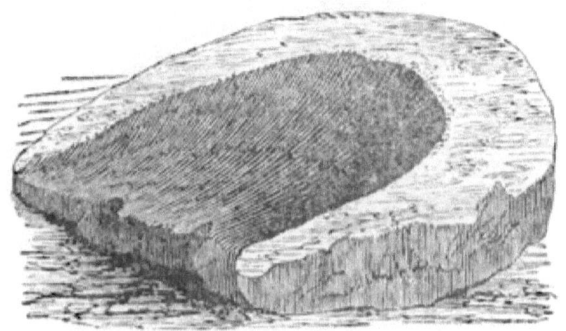

Rude Granite Mill.

(C) in the plan, "2 feet 6 inches long, and about the same broad, set on its edge. On its south side were a number of small loose stones; on the north side, at D, lay many calcined human bones, fragments of a large urn, and a small one entire, mouth downwards, filled with soil."

From the drawing of it, given on the next page, the reader may justly compare this little urn, with that found at Trevello Karn. The pottery in this instance is, however, not so fine or well baked, the ornamentation is less regular, and there are no handles. From this it may be supposed to be a more ancient example of the same type.

MINIATURE URN, FROM BOSCAWEN-ÛN.
Height .... 4⅜ inches.
Diam. at mouth.................. 3½ inches.

It may be remarked, in conclusion, that the rock in the centre of this "Ring Barrow" is called the "Money" rock, which, for reasons which will be more apparent in the sequel, the author is inclined to believe, derives its name from the discovery, at some period or another of coins not far off.[1]

---

[1] In a note at a previous page, mention has been made of the occurrence in Cornwall of the Glain Neider, or Adder Beads. One of these, found on the Boscawen-ûn estate, is here figured.

ADDER'S BEAD—ACTUAL SIZE.

It is now preserved in the Penzance Natural History Museum, to which it was presented by Miss Carne. It is worthy of note, that this curious little

The engravings of the barrow and the mill-stone are taken from Mr. Blight's paper on the subject, appended to his beautiful little book of "Cornish Churches," a new edition of which is a great *desideratum* in the county.

CLAHAR GARDEN, MULLION.

URN FROM CLAHAR GARDEN.
FIG 1.

Height .... 1 foot.
Diam. at mouth .... 10½ inches.

---

glass ornament was found in the neighbourhood of the circle and barrows just described. The glass is of a blueish colour, the wavy line which surrounds it being yellow. T. Q. Couch, Esq., F.S.A., has kindly communicated the account of one of these curious little beads, now in his possession, found *in a stone cairn*, near Fowey. It is remarkable to find that these beads, about which local traditions still exist in more than one part of Great Britain, are actually found in connection with the ancient sepulchral remains.

The four Urns, figured in this notice, were recently taken from a barrow on the estate called Clahar Garden, the property of Lord Robartes, in the parish of Mullion. Mr. Thomas, who farms the estate, had occasion to remove the cairn, thirty-six feet in diameter, in which they were found, for agricultural purposes.

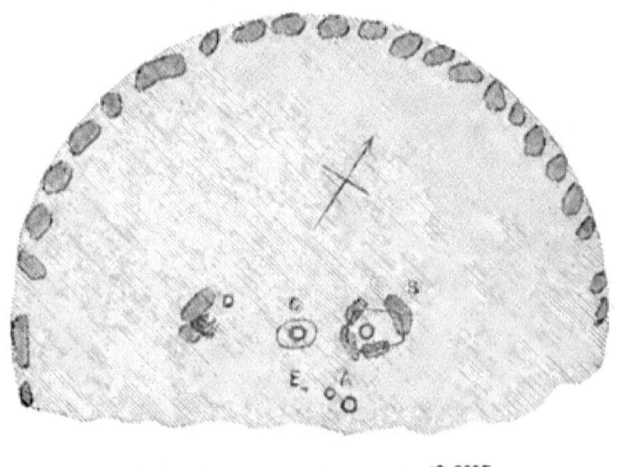

PLAN OF THE BARROW.

Passing the outer ring of stones, the workmen discovered the Urns in the following positions, (which will be better understood by referring to the plan than by any other mode of description).

Figs. 1 and 3 were found at A. Both these were broken in pieces, but enough fragments remained to permit of their restoration in the shape of the drawings here given. Whether they were contained in a Kist-Vaen is unfortunately unrecorded.

Fig. 2 was at B, four stones being placed round it, and one flat one on the top. The mouth was downwards, resting on a flat stone.

Fig. 4 was found at C, under a flat stone, at a distance of 1 foot 6 inches from the Kist-Vaen which contained figure 2, and two feet from A, where the

FIG. 3.　　　　　FIG. 2.　　　　　FIG. 4.
THREE URNS FROM CLAHAR GARDEN.

FIG. 2.
Height .... 6¼ inches.
Diam. at mouth .... 4⅜ inches.

FIG. 3.
Height .... 4⅞ inches.
Diam. at top .... 4¾ inches.

FIG. 4.
Height .... 3½ inches.
Diam. at top .... 4 inches.

others were found. Of the flints found at the same time, Fig. 1 was discovered at E, apart from either of the urns; Fig. 2 at B, with the ashes contained in the urn; and Fig. 3, with a quantity of ashes lying by the side of two stones, set in some order, at D, five feet south-west of C, where the urn marked Fig. 4 was found.

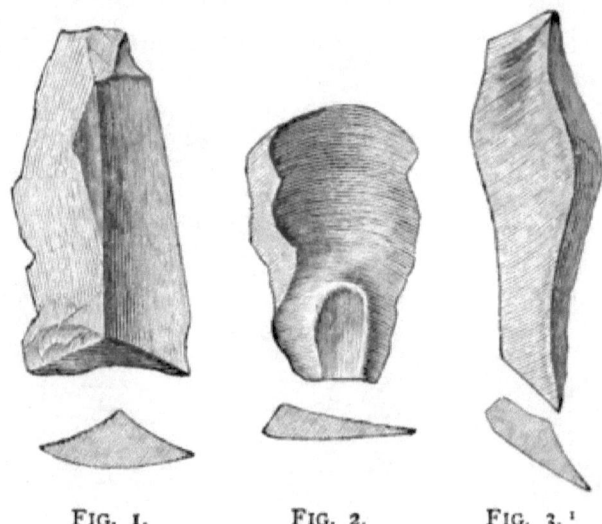

FIG. 1.   FIG. 2.   FIG. 3.[1]
THREE FLINTS FROM CLAHAR GARDEN BARROW.
From a Drawing by Mr. Blight.

It is greatly to be regretted that circumstances have prevented a more detailed account of this most interesting barrow from being placed on record. The accurate and invaluable MS. drawings by Mr. J. T. Blight, F.S.A., have supplied the author with the means of presenting the reader with the above engravings. The drawings Mr. Blight made on the

---

[1] The flints themselves are unfortunately mislaid.

spot ; and he himself superintended the greater part of the work of exploration. His present state of health, which precludes him from prosecuting those pursuits in which he so greatly excelled, must be regarded as a subject of deep regret by all who were acquainted with his works, but more especially by those who were personally acquainted with him.

The pattern which surrounds the urn marked Fig. 2 must not be passed over without a remark. It is the only instance which Cornwall affords of anything like an attempt at imitation of natural phenomena on the ancient sepulchral pottery.[1] It seems, indeed, highly probable that many of the indented patterns on pottery, such as that from West Kennet, do in reality represent vegetable matter of some sort. The idea that, in its origin, the chevron pattern represented the basket frame-work used in early times to support the clay, although a happy one, is capable of being overstrained, especially if applied to pottery of comparatively recent times. The same might, perhaps, be said of the notion that this pattern originated in ferns, (used either in the funeral pyre, or in the formation of the pottery,) becoming pressed against, or imbedded in the clay while wet.

---

[1] Mr. Bateman has gone so far as to say that no imitations of natural objects are found among any of the Celtic pottery; but this, perhaps, regards their shape rather than their ornamentation.

Yet, that a double row of leaves shooting off from a central stem, and bearing a strong resemblance to the fern, is the intention in the case of this Clahar Garden Urn, no one can doubt, who looks at the vessel. It will be seen that each of the diagonal lines, forming the limbs of the chevron, has its extremity twisted round so as to meet the next one, giving a long leaf-shaped figure; while a horizontal line, carried round the vessel, forms the stem from which these leaves shoot out on either side.

The pottery at Clahar Garden was distinguished by a ruddy-brown appearance. The single urn,[1] Fig. 2, which is still perfect, bears an unmistakable resemblance in pattern and in form to those found at Trevello and Boscawen-ûn.

PENQUITE.

The next sepulchral urn, with a drawing of which the reader is here presented, was found many years ago at or near Penquite, on the Fowey river.

---

[1] The two other small urns (Figs. 3 and 4) are very like those discovered by Mr. C. Hall, in Rough Barrow, on Chiselbourne Common, Dorset. One of these was "*full of small birds' bones.*" See "*The Barrow Diggers,*" Pl. 9, p. 92.

In form it is not unique, but it is so different from any other in this work, that it is the more to be regretted that no description of the discovery should

Sepulchral Urn at Penquite.—Height uncertain.

have been preserved. The above sketch was made by the late Canon Rogers, who observes, in a note appended to it, that "from the elegance of the form, neatness of the workmanship, the firmness and hardness of the pottery, and from its having been evidently turned," he supposes it to be Roman.[1]

---

[1] In shape and ornamentation this vessel is precisely similar to one found at Droitwich, and figured in Mr. Allies' *Antiquities of Worcestershire*. "In the adjacent soil," says Mr. Allies, "were found remains of a human skeleton." "It was found at a depth of three or four feet, at Mr. Ellins' salt works," near which spot a Roman tesselated pavement was subsequently discovered. Another similar vessel is reported to have been found *with Roman remains* near Bagshot. The Droitwich vessel was 6 inches high.

SENNEN.

URN FROM SENNEN.
Height .... 5¾ inches.

The above little urn, which has all the characteristics of Roman, or Romano British manufacture, both in texture and shape, was presented to the Truro Museum by the late Rev. John Buller. The paper attached to it, only states that it was "found at Sennen."

Mr. Davies Gilbert *(History of Cornwall,* vol. i, p. 193,) says, that about the year 1801, "a cave was discovered near the Land's End, in which was an urn, containing ashes, bones, and brass coins." Four of these were in Mr. Gilbert's possession.

This may possibly allude to the same discovery, since, from the form of the above vessel, it is almost certain that it belongs to a late period.

TREDINNEY.

THE TREDINNEY URN.
Height.................................... 12 inches.
Diam. at mouth........................ 9 inches.

Six miles west of Penzance, on the brow of a hill on the right-hand side of the road leading to the Land's End, was an undisturbed cairn, thirty-eight feet in diameter, mounted on a pile of natural rocks, and surrounded by a ring of sixteen large granite blocks set on edge. On the 21st of August, 1868, the author proceeded with some miners to the spot, and caused an oblong trench to be sunk across the centre of the mound. About eighteen inches from the surface, was a pile of rocks, (the natural formation of the crest of the hill,) as will be seen by the accompanying plan. One of the largest of these

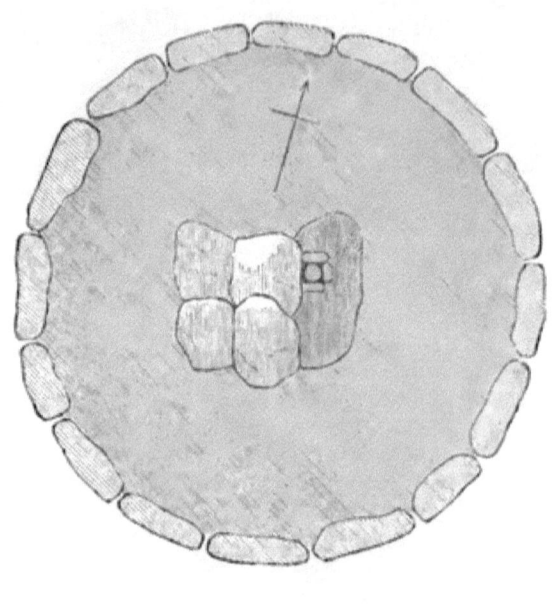

PLAN OF THE TREDINNEY BARROW.

rested diagonally upon the others, the slope being towards the eastern side. Following the slope of this stone, (on which the body was no doubt reduced to ashes,) a flat stone, three feet long by two feet broad, was presently reached, one end of which was resting against the sloping rock. Under this was a Kist-Vaen, one foot in length, 1 foot 4 inches in breadth, and eighteen inches deep, constructed of eight stones in two layers of four each. These side-stones had been purposely fitted closely in round the urn, which was in this manner so tightly wedged that the stones had to be removed in order to extricate it. It stood, mouth downwards, on a turf, which, in turn, rested on a flat natural rock.

The vessel was filled with bones, among which were two chipped flints. Two more flints were found outside the urn, but within the kist. The pottery, which is of a brownish colour, is sufficiently, though not well baked; it is ornamented with the usual chevron pattern, placed horizontally, as on the Clahar

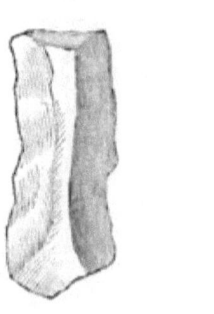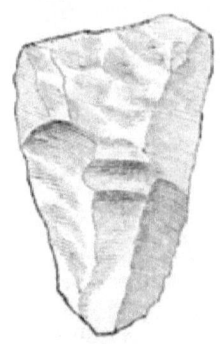

Flints from Tredinney.

Garden Urns. What seemed strange was, that the vessel had no bottom; and as it is not likely that that part would have decayed sooner than the rest, it is reasonable to suppose that it was broken off in order to allow the ashes from the sloping rock to be swept into it. There are four pierced bosses or handles, as on the Gerrans Urn.

The bones found in the Urn were not so completely calcined as is usually the case. They were identified as those of a delicately made man, or more probably of a woman. The sloping rock in the centre of the barrow was surrounded on all sides with ashes and charred wood; and, beneath it, when raised, was nearly a cartload of ashes, as white and fresh as if the fire had scarcely been extinguished from them.

On this same farm of Tredinney was discovered, a short time since, a gold ornament of a semicircular form, evidently part of one of those ornaments known as small torques or British ring-money.

ANGROWSE, MULLION.
First Barrow.

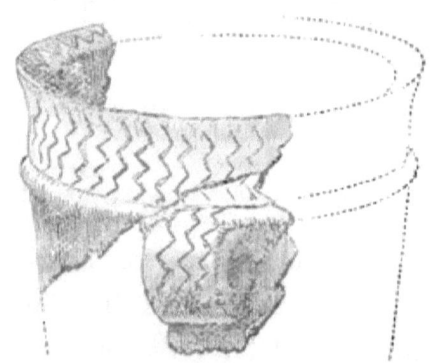

The Angrowse Urn. No. 1.
Height..................................... Uncertain.
Diam. at mouth .... 12¼ inches.

It is one of the characteristics of Cornish Barrows,

that they are very frequently met with on the cliffs. Indeed, the words of Beowulf might often have been well applied to the Cornu-Britons:—

> "Then wrought
> The people of the Westerns
> A mound over the sea.
> It was high and broad
> By the sea-faring man
> To be seen afar."

The Cliffs on the western coast of the Lizard promontory, and those in the parish of Mullion in especial, afford many examples of this practice.

Mr. Williams, the proprietor of the estate called Angrowse, had been carrying the extensive improvements on his farm to the very edge of the cliff. In doing so, it was necessary to remove a circular pile of stones about thirty-five feet in diameter, and three or four in height. This heap or ring had a considerable depression in the centre. During its removal, nothing remarkable occurred until the workmen came to the western side, when they laid bare two layers of flat stones covering a pit (four feet long by two feet broad), cut in the hard natural soil to a depth of about two feet. In taking the earth from this pit, they soon discovered the fragments of the urn (figured on p. 234), a bronze dagger, with three rivets, and a fractured globular specimen of mundick, or iron-pyrites. Only the upper portions of the vessel could be found; and many of the fragments were in such a rotten state, owing to the wet which had accumulated in the pit, that it is almost certain that the rest of it had become entirely decomposed. From the fragments preserved, it appears that the indented chevron pattern extended, in perpendicular zigzag lines, round the upper portions of the vessel in a band three inches wide; that it was continued over two perforated handles, two inches wide, and one-and-a-half inches in relief, and that the same pattern, placed horizontally, adorned the inner part of the upper rim. The pottery, which is unusually well baked, is full of gravel, and was originally of a reddish colour, though some portions of it are much blackened by fire. In general appearance this urn resembles that found at Boleit.

The bronze dagger measures six-and-three-quarter inches in length, and is another example of a type

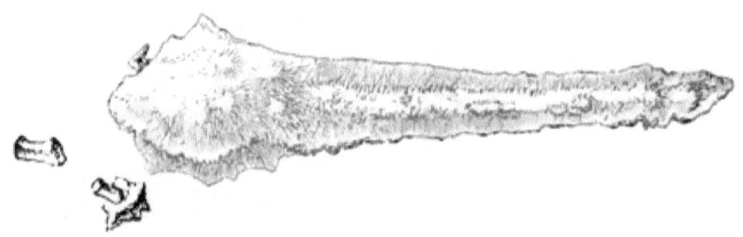

BRONZE DAGGER FROM ANGROWSE.

frequently found in connection with Cornish interments. The piece of mundick is one-and-a-half inches in diameter, and the neat angular fracture made in it shows signs of friction, as if something had been sharply struck against it, or rapidly and continuously drawn through it. It may, therefore, be reasonably supposed that it was in some way connected with striking the light for the funeral pile.[1] Many calcined bones were found throughout the pit.

ANGROWSE, MULLION.
Second Barrow.

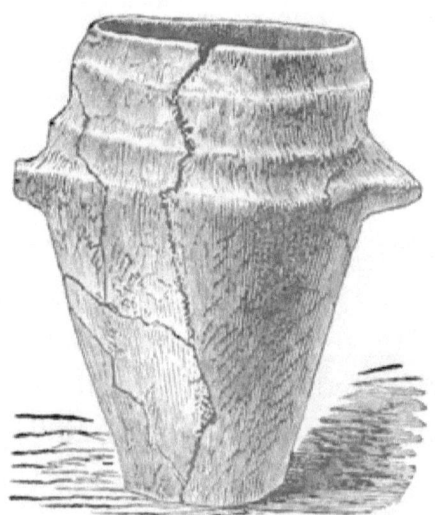

THE ANGROWSE URN.   NO. 2.

Height .... 16 inches.
Diam. at mouth .... 10 inches.

The former discovery at Angrowse having been

---

[1] For an elaborate account of pyrites, used for obtaining light, see *Ancient Stone Implements*, by John Evans, Esq., F.R.S., p. 281.

kindly made known to the author by J. J. Rogers, of Penrose, Esq., he proceeded to the place a few days afterwards. To Mr. Williams, the freeholder of the property, he must here tender his best thanks both for the information he afforded him with reference to the first barrow, and also for his courtesy and kindness in lending his own labourers to assist in the exploration of a second barrow, also on the cliff, some three or four hundred yards distant from the one just described. Unlike that one, however, this mound was highest in the centre, and *entirely* composed of earth. It had a diameter of thirty feet, and was from three to four feet high. A thin flat stone was soon reached, lying in the centre of the barrow a few inches above the natural level of the ground. Under this, the rim of an urn appeared, standing mouth upwards. It is remarkable how exceedingly rude the interment in this case turned out to be. A pit had been excavated in the natural soil sufficiently large to receive the lower part of the vessel, which is of the vase type,[1] and tapers towards the bottom. Two rude bosses or handles protruding from the sides had prevented the urn from sinking to the bottom of the pit; and while it was thus suspended, (its rim being above the surface of the soil), a narrow slate stone had been placed on its mouth, not suffi-

---

[1] Like that at Tresvenneck, see page 104.

ciently large to cover the aperture. The barrow had been then raised over the whole; and, as might be expected, the urn was broken in pieces, and not without great difficulty could it be restored to its original shape, as seen at p. 237. It was filled up to the brim with ashes and human bones, the latter not so much burnt as those found in the other barrow.[1] The pottery is extremely rude and ill burnt; the bands or ridges round the upper part being very irregular. One of the protuberances or handles, (omitted apparently at first,) had been subsequently baked harder than the rest of the vessel, and stuck on as an afterthought. In colour the exterior is of a yellowish grey, but the interior is blackened by fire. The contents were doubtless placed in the vessel while still burning.

The only attempt at ornamentation is made by some forty or fifty indentations round the rim, made with *the point of the finger nail* while the clay was wet. Altogether, this is the rudest and probably the most primitive urn yet discovered in Cornwall, and the interment the most careless and barbarous. It would seem to be of much earlier date than the first barrow; and, if so, it might be argued that the vase-shaped vessels, such as this one, and those from Tresvenneck, and Brane Common, are of an earlier

---

[1] These bones are believed to be those of a woman.

date than the cylindrical ones, which latter are by far the most common.

At Tremenee, the adjoining farm to Angrowse, is a cave similar to that at Chapel Euny, and another is said to exist not far from the spot where these urns were found.

PRADANACK, MULLION.

The barrow just described, was opened on the 22nd of September, 1871; and on the 11th of November following, the author formed one of a party to explore another mound, situated on the Pradanack estate, two miles south of Angrowse. The tumulus in this instance was about four feet in height, and had a diameter of forty-two feet. It was surrounded by a ring of stones set on edge; but otherwise, was entirely composed of earth. At a depth of scarcely three feet in the exact centre, the pickaxe struck into a substance much harder than the rest of the mound. This turned out to be a bed of white clay, common to the country around, which had been artificially heaped up as a protection to a quantity of calcined bones and ashes. This deposit, on being uncovered, presented a most curious appearance. There being no covering stone, the fibres and roots from the surface had found their way to the bones. These had been originally contained in a small urn, but the roots had caused them to expand, and to burst the vessel. The conglomerate, when removed, measured about nine inches in thickness by 1 foot 6 inches in diameter; it had much the appearance and quite the consistency of hard Cavendish tobacco; and round the edges of the mass were found adhering the small broken fragments of the vessel, which, to the otherwise unprotected ashes, had served the purpose of a kist. The urn must have been of the cylindrical shape, about seven inches high. It was carelessly baked, but ornamented with the chevron pattern placed perpendicularly, like a succession of the letters V, under which was a line of dotted indentations, not unlike those on the Morvah Hill example, to be presently described.

There are several barrows on the cliff in this estate, which appear to have been all previously cut through.

The author's thanks are due to Mr. Blight, senr., for directing his attention to the Pradanack mound, as well as to many other Lizard Antiquities.

DENZELL DOWNS, near St. COLUMB.

In the summer of 1871, the author took up his quarters at the Red Lion Hotel, in St. Columb, (by the way, one of the most comfortable houses in the

West of England), for the purpose of exploring some of the numerous barrows scattered over the Downs

THE DENZELL URN—(RESTORED).
From a Drawing by the Author.

in that neighbourhood. Through the kind instrumentality of his landlord, Mr. Polkinghorne, he was not only enabled to discover the whereabouts of these antiquities, but also to obtain the requisite permission to investigate their contents.

Any one, referring to the Ordnance Survey, will

perceive that the waste lands in the parishes of St. Eval, St. Ervan, and St. Breock, are strewn with tumuli, sometimes placed singly on the tops of the hills, sometimes running in lines, of eight or nine together, over the downs. But, numerous though they are, their contents seldom repay the explorer for his trouble. Some eight or nine, though dug through with the utmost care, presented no results whatever. One bowl barrow (they are generally of this shape,) on the estate of Carnhewas, the property of Mr. Drew, seven feet in height and sixty in diameter, yielded only the crushed remains of a domestic vessel, of the narrow-mouthed Roman type, at a depth of four feet from the surface. Another on the Carnecledgy Downs, the property of John Michael Williams, Esq., three miles to the eastward of the former, though perfectly untouched before, was found to contain nothing but a pile of loose stones under its superstratum of earth. Two small ones, on the hill above the farm called Borlase, were equally unprofitable; and two more in the centre of the entrenchments at Castle-an-dinas seemed to have been opened before.[1]

Perseverance was, however, to be rewarded. On Denzell Downs are five large barrows, three of which lie in a line bearing N. and S.; while the line of the

---

[1] Many barrows in this vicinity were opened by the late Rev. Sir Hugh Molesworth, but without any noteworthy result. A spear-head is said to have occurred in one at Penatilly.

other two cuts it diagonally in a direction N.N.E. and S.S.W. These tumuli average from seventy to ninety feet in diameter, and from seven to twelve feet in height. All seem to have been surrounded by a ring of stones, though in one or two instances it has been covered up or removed.

Two years since, Mr. Capell, the farmer at Denzell, while ploughing round the tumulus nearest his house, discovered a large urn close to the surface at the exterior of the mound. This vessel, he asserts, stood between two and three feet high, and judging from the fragments, (restored in the sketch on p. 242), it cannot have been much less. The horizontal and perpendicular lines with which it is ornamented are clearly made by the pressure of a twisted cord upon the wet clay. The pottery is remarkably heavy, and is baked very hard and black throughout. In some places it is more than an inch thick. In the urn were burnt bones, and a bronze "knife," which, from the description, was probably a weapon of the same class as those found at Benallack, Angrowse, and Pelynt.[1]

On Wednesday, July 12th, 1871, some workmen were employed by the author to dig a trench through the centre of the barrow next in the line to that in

---

[1] The Rev. Mr. Kirwan, F.S.A., found a similar one in a barrow on Broad Down, Devon, (See *Trans. Dev. Assoc.*, vol. iv, p. 302); he also found a socketed celt in a Kist-Vaen on the same downs. (*Comp.*, p. 5, *ante*).

which this urn was found, being the middle barrow of the three. This mound was eighty feet in diameter, and about nine in height. It was composed of the surface ground of the neighbourhood, and, like that previously noticed at Pelynt, contained several strata of differently coloured soil. At the depth of five feet in the exact centre, lay a deposit of very small chippings of burnt bone and ashes, about a quart in all, amalgamated with the yellow clay. Three feet west of this, and on the same level, was another vein of bone splinters. Both these interments had been placed there at the same time as the rest of the mound, since there was no sign of subsequent disturbance in the strata above them.

Three feet N.E. of the first find, and at a depth of nine feet from the top of the tumulus, lay a large deposit of burnt bone and ashes. A slight pit had been made for it in the solid ground, but no Kist-Vaen, side stones, or cover protected it from the weight of the surrounding soil. On nearing the spot where this deposit lay, the pick-axe cut suddenly into a cavity in the ground.[1] The bones in all would have filled between two and three quarts, and lying in their midst, mouth upwards, and serving as the

---

[1] This fact leads to the supposition that a wooden or wicker framework, now decayed, originally served the purpose of a kist.

receptacle for some of them, was the curious little cup here figured:—

THE DENZELL CUP.
Height .... 3 and 1-5th inches.
Diam. at mouth .... 4 inches.

With regard to this little vessel, Mr. Albert Way, in a letter to the author on the subject, informs him that, although "round-bottomed cups of amber and of bituminous shale presenting the peculiarity of one small handle[1] or ear have occurred in barrows, and although there are also a few instances of such vessels of clay, much decorated with scored markings, yet none of them is identical with this one." The small clay cups referred to by Mr. Way are sometimes found in Ireland, and generally will not stand upright. This is not the case with the Denzell cup, which, although round at the bottom, is well balanced when

---

[1] See *Trans. of the Devonshire Assoc.*, vol. ii, p. 619.

placed on end. Although it contained human bones, there was no sign of fire about it, as there invariably is in the case of the other Cornish sepulchral vessels. Externally the clay is of a ruddy hue, but the interior presents a coating of yellow. The pottery is rough and gravelly, but well baked. In thickness it averages from two-tenths to three-tenths-of-an-inch. The lip seems conveniently formed for drinking, and from this circumstance, as well as from the size and shape of the little vessel, it may be supposed that such was its original purpose; and that it was only used as a receptacle for the bones, because no more fitting vessel came to hand at the moment, in which, according to custom, to deposit them. A turf had been placed on its mouth.

MORVAH HILL.

The natural granite ridge, known as Trevean or Morvah Hill, is surmounted by numerous mine burrows, among which may easily be distinguished three genuine sepulchral cairns, or rather, it may be, two cairns and a beacon. One cairn crowns the south-western end of the hill, the other the north-eastern. These two are several hundred yards apart; while "the beacon," or artificial heap of stones raised round a natural rock, is situated only thirty paces from the north-eastern one. In the summer of

1863, the author proceeded to investigate these remains. Hearing that the north-eastern cairn had been previously rifled by a party of surveyors who pitched their tent in the midst of the stone ring, he commenced an attack upon "the beacon," thinking

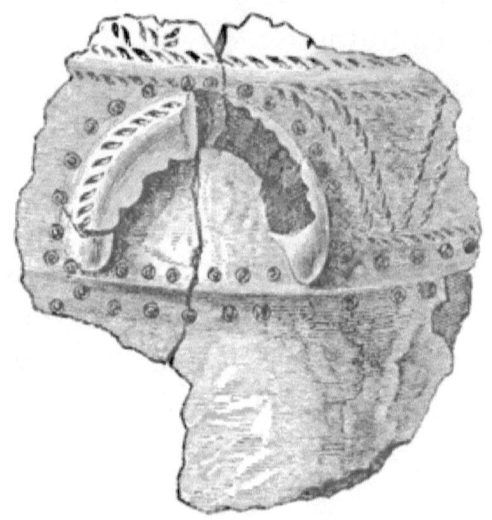

FRAGMENT OF THE MORVAH HILL URN.
Height of fragment .... 5 inches.

it might be a barrow of some sort. Failing, however, to find the place of interment, this was also abandoned for the third and last. It proved to be a pile of loose stones, raised on a base of natural rock, and enclosed by a ring of twenty stones set on edge, fitted together lengthways with unusual precision and care. The diameter of the barrow, which is nearly a perfect circle, is twenty-nine feet. Unlike the ordinary stone circles round Cornish barrows, this one was originally constructed of several layers of stones fitted together, one over the other, without mortar, forming, as it seemed, a cone over the entire tumulus, similar in style and contrivance to the British beehive-huts. A similar mode of cairn-building occurs in one of three tumuli on Sharp Tor, near Liskeard; and among the ancient sepulchres of Algeria, it seems to be an ordinary and recognised form.[1]

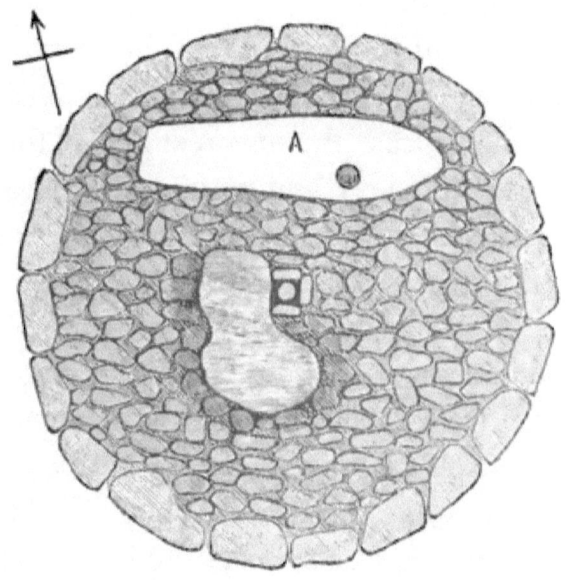

PLAN OF THE MORVAH HILL BARROW.

---

[1] "De Septentrionalibus populis refert Christianus Cilicius belli Dithmarsici lib. I. 'Erant eorum sepulturæ in silvis et agris, tumulosque *aggestis lapidibus vestientes muniebant*, quod genus complures passim adhuc visuntur, qui gigantum strata vocantur.'" *J. A. Quenstedt, Sep. Vet.* p. 190. This may refer to a similar practice.

Within the ring on the northern side, as may be seen by the plan, lies a large natural rock (A) at present uncovered. At the eastern extremity of this rock is a small circular cavity, four or five inches deep, which, from the appearance of the granite, seems due to artificial, rather than natural causes. The rock itself was resting at each end on the natural soil, from which it had never been removed; but a pit had been sunk, as was afterwards found, immediately underneath it.

Sinking a shaft in the centre of the barrow, at the depth of about eight feet the workmen arrived at two natural granite rocks, the one resting on the other, (just as at Tredinney) and sloping downwards towards its eastern end. This slanting rock was about four feet square; and when found was covered with a black, slimy substance. This being removed, a small artificial cavity was observed in the upper end of the stone, from which a narrow trench could be traced down the sloping surface. Following this trench, a flat stone was soon reached, three feet square. Under this was a Kist-Vaen about eighteen inches deep, (formed as usual of four side-stones,) in which stood an urn, mouth upwards.[1]

On the cover-stone being first raised, the urn was

---

[1] The urn was unfortunately broken by the workman placing his foot upon the earth in the pit.

not perceived; but upon the top of the earth in the kist, on which the stone had been resting, lay a third-brass Roman coin, in a state of semi-decomposition, the substance of it being more like clay slate than metal. Several other coins were found in the Kist-Vaen, and on the obverse of one, a middle brass, is a laureated head to the right, with the legend CONSTAN[1] very plain. Another bears the head and shoulders of a soldier helmeted, with the shield below, from the disc of which protrudes the point of a spear. This is a type well known on the coins of the later Emperors, and, like the first, probably belongs to some member of the Constantine family. It may be as well to state at once that from the position of these coins, their distance from the surface, and the construction of the kist itself, it is quite impossible that by any means they could have reached the situation in which they were found after the covering stone had been once set in its place.[2]

The urn appears to have been, when perfect, a small vessel, of the usual cylindrical shape, rising from a bottom of five inches diameter. It is well baked, though the pottery is thick and rude, and the

---

[1] The rest of the legend is obliterated, and the head is also indistinct. The author at first believed it to be a Constantius, but a more careful examination proves it to be Constantine the Great. A.D. 274-337.

[2] This fact alone, (even were it a single instance,) is enough to throw back the *onus probandi* on those who deny the Post-Roman origin of some at least of the Cornish "Cairns."

exterior still wears the original yellow colour of the clay.

Its ornamentation is, as will be seen, the ordinary chevron pattern, placed perpendicularly between doubled lines of indentations, below which are two rows of small round holes, some of them sunk to one-twentieth-of-an-inch in the clay. This pattern is varied by semicircular embossed ornaments in high relief, serving, no doubt, for holdfasts or handles. A precedent for this unusual type will be found in the fragment of pottery from Duloe circle, engraved at page 128. The bones contained in the urn were so thoroughly calcined that they adhered like white cement to the interior of the vessel.

Under the slanting rock in the centre of the barrow were a few more bones and a limpet-shell. Quantities of ashes, burnt stones, a few pebbles, and charred wood, were scattered throughout the mound.

On examining the bones taken from the urn, a small flint disc, struck from a pebble, was discovered. Similar chips are common to the surface of the neighbouring downs.

The Age of the Monuments.

"1st. BARROW DIGGER.
'Give me leave. Here is a Common; good; here is the Barrow; good; if the Barrow contains Roman Arms, or Urns, it must be a Roman Barrow; mark you that.'"

The Barrow Diggers.
A Dialogue.

S the ultimate purpose of all Antiquarian research is, as was stated at the outset, to affix a date to each and every object of which it takes account, it now only remains to be seen what evidence the preceding pages may have afforded on the subject of the age of the Monuments therein described.

Hitherto the essay has been simply descriptive; the only deviations from this rule being the few remarks upon the comparative antiquity of Kist-Vaens and Tripod Cromlechs; and the practices of Inhumation and Cremation. No proposition has been given to be worked out; no skeleton theory to be filled in; and the author may freely confess, that when he commenced his researches among the ancient Cornish sepulchres a few years since, he had no theory whatever to offer on the subject of their age.

With the works of Nillson and Sir John Lubbock before him, he was rather, if anything, impressed with the notion that they all belonged to the remote irrecoverable past; and it was not until he came to reflect on the consequences involved in the discovery, just narrated, at Morvah Hill, and to compare it with other finds in the same district, that he arrived at the conclusion that some at least of the most typical of the interments might be brought within historic times, and assigned to the early centuries of the Christian era. The importance of finding a coin in such a situation as that at Morvah Hill needs no comment. It marks a period, *anterior* to which the deposit cannot be. On the other hand, however, it by no means settles the question of how long a time may have elapsed between its coinage and its interment in the urn in which it was found. It is probable, although by no means a point to be insisted on, that these brass coins of the later

Emperors served, in the absence of native money, the purposes of traffic among the Britons, long after the Romans had departed. This view of the case is rendered probable, first, from the vast number that were coined; second, from the evidences of a lengthy circulation which their worn and defaced state often indicates; and, third, from their not unusual occurrence in England in company with those coins of the Lower Empire which were certainly in use in Western Europe a few centuries later.

The proportion in which coins of the several Roman Emperors and Tyrants have been found in Cornwall, does not materially differ from that of other parts of England. Stray coins of the earlier Emperors *have* been found, but these are few and far between. With the age of the Antonines the proportion greatly increases; but it is not until the middle of the third century that they appear in any considerable quantities.

From Gallienus (260 A.D.) down to Valentinian, a century later, all the *hordes* of coins date. Among the more common are those of Postumus; Victorinus; Tetricus, sen. and jun.; Claudius Gothicus; Aurelian; Tacitus; Probus; and the family of Constantine. Mr. Buller, in his *History of St. Just*, mentions the remarkable fact that coins of Carausius (usually scarce) are common in that parish.

Unfortunately there is no period of the British

Annals involved in such impenetrable darkness as that during which these very coins were in circulation. From the absolute silence of the chroniclers, Lingard infers that the seventy years which succeeded the death of Severus "were years of tranquility and happiness." But, while it is true that the Northern tribes may have been held in check by the strength of the new fortification, there seems to have been nothing to overawe the southern portion of the *ferox provincia;* and a maritime district, such as Cornwall, remote from the main road of the legions from Gaul to the North, can scarcely, in those lawless times, have escaped being frequently the stronghold of some marauding chief; if not, of one of those petty tyrants, such as Carausius himself, whose claims were just then convulsing the empire of the world. In fact, the more accustomed the eye of the historian or of the antiquary becomes to the darkness of this period, the more readily will it distinguish scenes, not of peace and prosperity, but of bloodshed and rapine.

The wilder portions of Western Danmonia, from Dartmoor to the Land's End, bear evident traces of having once been the theatres of military operations offensive and defensive. Earthworks on the hills and cliffs mark the camps of the invaders, and the retreats of the invaded, while the cairns or tumuli, and (if Dr. Fergusson be right) the circles and avenues, scattered over the "bare and broken heather," no less truly denote the spot

> "Whence the angry soul ascended
> To the judgment-seat of God."

Interspersed, however, with these monuments of unrecorded misery lie the ruinous heaps of what were once the dwellings of a large resident population. To the cultivation of grain the mildness of the climate was favourable, and thus in close proximity to these hut-villages it is usual to find plots of ground, artificially levelled and cleared of stones. The daily consumption was taken from the unthrashed corn, preserved in caves under the huts, which also served as refuges for the inhabitants, when the winter was severe, or danger threatened.

The mills in which this corn was ground were of the rudest possible kind, consisting of granite blocks scooped out on one side. In these hollow basins, mullars, consisting generally of sea-worn stones, averaging from two feet to six inches in diameter, were worked by the hand. Cattle were also kept in considerable numbers in these villages, as appears by the numerous stone pens which accompany the huts. The dwellings themselves were either circular or oblong; but almost invariably built in the beehive manner, that is, of layers of stone overlapping each other until they approach sufficiently near for a single

R

slab to complete the roof. Sometimes the group of structures was surrounded by an embankment of stone or earth; sometimes it was placed so close to a "hill-castle," that a retreat of a few hundred yards would place the families and their goods in safety; sometimes a cave, built in the same beehive style, formed part of the group, serving, as before observed, for the *suffugium hiemi et receptaculum frugibus.*[1]

In their structure these huts are doubtless of native origin, and have their counterpart in the 'Picts Houses' of Scotland, as well as in Irish examples. Their occupation, however, as far as Cornwall is concerned, dates from Romano-British times. Of this fact, the following discoveries made in some of them, may be considered as very good evidence.

1. At Carnbrè, near Redruth. In one of the many circular huts on this hill was found a pint of Roman coins; the head of an animal in brass, etc. Two of these coins figured by Borlase are, respectively, those of *Tetricus senior*, and the *Urbs Roma* type.[2] [An excellent paper on the subject of the fortified hut town on Carnbrè has been drawn up by Sir Gardner Wilkinson, and will be found in the *Report of*

---

[1] Tacitus on the Caves of the Germans. *Germania, Ch.* xvi.
[2] *Antiquities of Cornwall*, Edit. i, 288, and pl. v.

the Royal Institution of Cornwall, for the year 1860. Gold Celtic coins were found "on the ridge" of Carnbrè, in June, 1749, and are engraved by Borlase. *Ant. of Cornwall,* pl. xix. Bronze celts *in company with Roman coins,* viz: Antoninus Pius, Severus Alexander, and Constantius, were taken in 1744 from the side of this same "fruitful hill." *Id,* page 263.]

2. At Bodinar Crellas, in Sancred parish. This group of huts is ranged round the southern and eastern slope of Bodinar Hill. It is not surrounded by any rampart, but from its position, must have been a place of considerable strength. Within the memory of man a subterranean passage was to be found at this place, as also two beehive huts with lintels over the doors. The most perfect of those huts whose foundations can still be made out, measures forty-two feet by thirty-five in diameter, is of an oval form, and is surrounded by smaller huts opening into it. On two separate occasions, deposits of Roman third brass coins have been found in connection with this beehive village. The first was accompanied by pottery, ashes, a stone bowl, and a mullar; the second and larger deposit was taken from under a flat stone at the entrance of the enclosure. Out of this latter horde, three, secured by the author,

proved to be those of Tetricus, jun., Victorinus, and Probus. Several others have been picked up in the adjacent fields.

THE LONG CHAMBER—CHAPEL EUNY CAVE.
(Reproduced by permission of the Society of Antiquaries).

3. At Chapel Euny. In a subterranean structure containing three long passages and a circular beehive hut, and running under a group of huts of similar construction on the surface, the author discovered in the year 1863, among other things, an iron spear-head, a crook and rivet of the same metal, a small perforated stone or spindle-whorl, a quantity of black pottery, bones of animals, and a piece of *Sa-*

mian ware.[1] [An account of the exploration of this cave will be found in the *Proceedings of the Society of Antiquaries of London,* for 1868.][2]

4. At Chigwidden. The fortified enclosure which bears this name is situated, like the two last-mentioned places, in the parish of Sancred. Immediately inside the rampart, an old man named Dennis found several small copper coins, which, from the account he gave of them to the author, were undoubtedly Roman third brass. Pottery, ashes, and mullars were also dug up in the same place. Within the memory of persons now living, there were small houses of the beehive kind in the centre of this enclosure; and a cave is said to have been discovered, roofed in with large slabs, in the next field.

To these four instances of late Roman remains, found in connection with the dwellings and forts of the ancient inhabitants of Cornwall, may be added the discoveries of coins of Antoninus near a subterranean structure at Boscaswell, in St. Just, and of uncertain Roman brass money in a circular enclosure at

---

[1] Compare the finds in Romano-British villages in other parts of Great Britain.

[2] Part of a granite mill-stone has been lately picked up here, and sent to the author by the farmer at Chapel Euny. It is an improvement upon the ruder ones usually found.

Morvah. A similar find was made at the Cliff-castle of Treryn, near the Logan Rock, and has been duly recorded by Leland; and, indeed, (were it necessary to do so), instances might be multiplied.

The hut dwellings and fortified enclosures being thus, from internal evidence, satisfactorily referred to a Romano-British occupation, the question may be asked: "where are the *sepulchres* of so considerable a population to be found?"

It is true that the cairns which invariably surmount the nearest available high ground seem to afford a tacit answer. Not, however, to jump at this conclusion without a fair amount of evidence, it will be necessary to name the following points of resemblance between the beehive huts and the tumuli. These consist: First, in the similarity of their general megalithic construction and arrangement:[1] Second, in the fact that the mill-stones and mullars used by the occupiers of the huts have also been found *deeply buried* among the stones composing the cairn:[2] Third, in the occurrence of the chevron, and indented linear patterns, on the pottery common to both:[3] and Fourth, in the dis-

---

[1] *e.g.* Barrows on Morvah Hill, and Sharp Tor, and indeed all the ring barrows; many of which have been mistaken for hut-dwellings.

[2] *e.g.* Boscawen-ûn and Rosemoddress Barrows.

[3] *e.g.* On the sepulchral pottery, passim. On the domestic, on that from Carne, in Zennor, and on a specimen in the Truro Museum.

covery of coins of the same age in both huts and tumuli.[1] Anyone who has taken the trouble to read carefully the descriptions in the previous pages of the explorations of the barrows, will at once remember the recurrence of the above points of resemblance, and will also recollect how frequently it has happened that tumuli, as well as megalithic monuments, have been found to be in close and convenient proximity to forts or beehive towns.

Perhaps of all the barrows above described, that on Morvah Hill is most worthy of a second notice. Here was an instance of an interment in a cairn, where the body had been burnt on a central natural rock surrounded by the usual ring of stones, the ashes placed in an urn of the usual chevron pattern, accompanied by the usual limpet and flint, protected by the usual Kist-Vaen, and finally covered in by the usual pile of stones. The whole arrangement, in short, being one of the most typical examples of the generality of barrows opened in the district. But here, in the very kist itself, what should appear but late Roman coins of the third century!

What is the most natural inference then? That the coins must be thrown out of the question, because of the flint chip? or the whole structure referred at

---

[1] *e.g.* Morvah Hill, Kerris, Goldvadnek, Karminchez, Ludgvan Barrows, Illogan, Carn Bré, Coswinsawson, (for the latter example see the coins of Constantine in the Truro Museum), &c., &c.

once to the Stone Age, thousands of years B.C., because it is encircled by large stones,[1] or because the pottery is rude, and its ornamentation not curvilinear?[2] Is it not rather the only fair course to admit at once that this interment, although possessing every characteristic of the so called Stone Age, was placed here not earlier than the end of the third century, A.D.; that is, at the time when the coin was struck.

But a comparison of the Morvah Hill Barrow and pottery with other finds in the neighbourhood proves to demonstration that it is only one out of a large number of interments, which owe their origin to one and the same funeral observances, and therefore presumably to one and the same people; and, approximately speaking, to one and the same age. If, therefore, the evidence as to date in the case of the Morvah Hill Barrow is considered conclusive, by far the greater number of the Cornish tumuli, and probably all the sepulchral pottery, must be handed over to Post-Roman times, and acknowledged as the genuine relics of the inhabitants of the beehive huts, and of those warriors who scaled or defended the ramparts on the hills.

But although a stand-point has thus been gained

---

[1] *Worsaae*, (Edit. Thoms.) p. 93.
[2] Sir John Lubbock. *Prehist. Times.* 2 Edit., p. 16.

with regard to the date of many individual tumuli, and a stepping stone as it were fixed in the abysmal gulf, it must still be remembered that, in many other cases, the extreme rudeness of the interments, *though accompanied by the same generally characteristic features*, betokens to all appearance a more remote period in the annals of the race. Either the urn is less carefully baked, or its ornamentation more rudely traced; or there is no urn at all, or perhaps no kist at all, only the deposit of splintered bone. Thus the difficult question arises, how many years may be allowed for the prevalence of a custom, such as that of placing a particular pattern on the vessels, or, indeed, of urn burial and incremation at all?

A careful comparison of the Cornish interments will only lead to the supposition that it must be reckoned by tens rather than by hundreds, and by hundreds rather than by thousands of years; and, while, on the one hand, it is extremely doubtful whether cremation was practised in Britain anterior to the contact of that nation with the Roman world; on the other, it must be remembered that as far as Cornwall is concerned, there are few, if any, instances of inhumation which can fairly be assigned to a period prior to that of the rude deposits of burnt bone-chips, such as have been found at the feet of the Menhirion.

It is true that in the case of the Trevelgue Barrow (see page 80,) an instance occurs of a class of interment whose Pre-Roman origin in the North of England Canon Greenwell has satisfied himself of; but, while acknowledging this to be the most ancient of our Cornish sepulchres, the fact must not be overlooked that in the same tumulus, and immediately above the kist containing the contracted body, a secondary interment had been deposited of the usual incinerated type. This mound was therefore recognised as a place of burial at the time when cremation was in vogue; and, just as in geology, the circumstance of one stratum overlying another implies (unless denudation has intervened,) immediate succession in point of age, so in the case of these two interments, it seems most probable that if their origin was not contemporaneous, no great distance of time can have elapsed between the deposition of the first and of the second.

From the extreme rarity of the earlier and contracted mode of burial when contrasted with the later and incinerated form, one inference may at all events be drawn, viz., that Cornwall was not a populous country until the time when it was inhabited by the people among whom the latter custom prevailed; that is, the author believes, until the early centuries of the Christian era. If before that time it possessed any considerable population, all that can be said is that "their memorial has perished with them." The reason of so great an influx of Celts at this period into a seemingly desolate land may be hard to account for; but the fact that such was the case is only the natural conclusion which an inspection and classification of the ancient sepulchres justifies the antiquary in arriving at.

The tendency to modernize these remains is by no means lessened when the Cromlechs are taken into consideration.

These stupendous edifices, "piled by the hands of Giants in the godlike days of old," have hitherto, in the popular mind at least, found their place in that great *supernatural*, which, with a total disregard to common sense, is always conveniently made to do duty in the case of every object about which nothing is known. To invest either a Jewish patriarch, or a Pre-Adamite savage with superhuman strength, is all very well. But some little evidence on the subject is required, when either the one or the other is said to be building a Cromlech. Without such proof, the further the monument can be drawn into a modern, and metallic age, the easier will it be to bring to the rescue the aid of such appliances, as would, without miracle, account for the erection of such grand and mysterious sarcophagi.

In all the larger Kist-Vaens, as has been remarked before, the graves are of sufficient size to have contained a body laid at length; and some by their shape seem to indicate that such was the intention of their builders. In one instance, however, (that at Bosporthennis) the author has himself taken up from the floor of the kist fragments of an urn of the late globular form, with ashes and burnt bone adhering to the inside. This may be set down to a secondary interment; but even then, those who placed it there must have recognized in the Cromlech a well known and not unusual form of sepulchre. Indeed, it is not at all unreasonable to suppose that Cromlechs are in many cases quite as late as the tumuli in which smaller Kist-Vaens are found. From this point of view the larger chamber would be regarded as the more elaborate form of the smaller, raised at the expense of greater labour in proportion to the honour due to the mightier dead.

A letter written by Mr. Tonkin to Bishop Gibson, on the 4th of August, 1733, and quoted by Dr. Borlase, p. 300 (edit. 2), gives a graphic, and, doubtless, a true description of the discovery of a Cromlech, with coins of a later date than any of the tumuli have hitherto produced. He says, "In 1702, in the parish of Tawednack, between St. Ies and the Land's End, were found under a prodigious rock of Moorstone called the Giant's Rock, a large flat stone supported by four pillars of the same, an Urn full of ashes with a round ball[1] of earth by the side of it, and in the said ball fourscore silver coins of the later Emperors, very fair and well preserved. I could not have the sight of more than five of them, of which I got three, of Valentinian I, Gratian, and Arcadius ; the rest were seized for the Lord of the Soil." MS. B., p. 224. To those who would apply the Danish theory to the Cornish Cromlechs, the author respectfully submits the above account as the most conclusive evidence to the contrary which it is possible to obtain.

But the proximity of the Cromlechs to the beehive huts and castles affords another reason for assigning them to the same period. Take the instance of Chywoone. Here is a Cromlech standing at a distance of only 250 paces from a hill castle, close to a British village, the castle itself containing foundations of huts, and the walls being formed of enormous blocks of granite, many of them larger than those of the neighbouring Kist-Vaen. What does this imply ? Either that the Cromlech is a more recent structure than the castle, or else that the

---

[1] Sir John Bowring has mentioned to the author a custom observed by him in Siam, curiously analogous to the above. On the death of the Queen of that country balls were made from the ashes of her funeral pile, in the centre of each of which a coin, belonging to her in her life-time, was placed. These balls were subsequently presented to her sorrowing friends. The author is indebted to Sir John for two of these balls which he has kindly placed in his collection.

builders of the castle allowed the Cromlech to remain unharmed while engaged in their work, and put themselves to the labour of obtaining stones from a greater distance, rather than disturb the structure. In the latter case the veneration which preserved the monument must have been due to the fact that it was either the grave of one of their own people, or of some one whose memory was at that time held in sufficient respect to save his tomb from desecration. Negative evidence of this kind is of course, when taken by itself, anything but satisfactory, but when considered in conjunction with the above-mentioned discoveries at Bosporthennis and Towednack, it goes far to validate the conclusion to which they so directly point.

There is one question in connection with the date of these interments which, from the prominence given it by the advocates of the primæval theory, must not be passed by without a comment. It is that of the flints; not of the carefully chipped or ground spear-heads, and barbed arrow-points of flint which are evidently works of art, and belong in some countries, such as Ireland, to a comparatively recent period; but those rough chips which, from their fractured forms and sharp edges, have obtained the names of "knives," "scrapers," &c. among modern writers in England, as well as on the continent. Before any argument is adduced from their presence in Cornish barrows, two questions must be asked and answered : —

First—Are they in reality of human manufacture?

Second—If indeed they are so, what evidence is there of their being *purposely* placed in the tumuli in which they occur?

With regard to the first of these questions, flints are certainly heterogeneous to the Cornish soil; therefore, they have been brought there.[1] The very great quantity in which the chips are found, strewn over the downs, leads to the doubt whether so great a traffic could ever have been maintained by human agency; and the glacial action, which sometimes imported such immense masses of rock into foreign and distant soils, has been brought into requisition to account for the phenomenon. Against this theory, it has been urged, (with what truth the author will not venture to say,) that the glacical action would be powerless to break these flints in the manner in which they are broken, and as it must be admitted that sea-washed flints are by no means uncommon on the Cornish coasts, it is possible that the inhabitants may have brought them thence to their chipping places, their dwellings, and their hearths, where, no doubt, they served, as indeed they have served

---

[1] See Sir H. De la Beche *Geology of Cornwall*, p. 429.

from the most primitive times down to the invention of matches, for the purpose of kindling the fire.

Secondly, then, allowing the possibility of their human origin, how far must it be supposed that they were *purposely* deposited *in the barrows*. In answer to this, it may be fairly said, that so common are they to certain districts, that it would be hard, even now, to raise a pile of earth skimmed off the surface, without flint chips being discoverable in it. Accident may, therefore, account for those that are not in immediate and seemingly intentional proximity to the interment. But accident, it must be added, can hardly account for those which occur, as many do, *in* the urns, *in* the kists, or mixed with the pile of ashes and charred wood. In these cases the author fully believes them to have afforded the means of kindling the fire which reduced the body to those ashes among which they are found.[1] The circular piece of mundick, cleft and worn in the centre, found at Mullion, and mentioned at page 236, he believes to have served a similar purpose.

This view of the case would amply account for all the finds of flint chips in *Cornish* barrows. The purpose they served in connection with *unburnt* remains in other countries must still remain a mystery;

---

[1] Mr. Evans, with his immense experience, has arrived at the same conclusion with regard to many specimens.

perhaps, in those cases they were strike-a-lights not for any torch in this world, but to guide the trembling soul in its way through the dusky valley to the distant "spirit-land."

In the course of these notes on the age of the Cornish sepulchres, any detailed comparison with those of other countries has been generally avoided, for the simple reason that if a particular district cannot bear testimony to the date of its own remains, it surely cannot borrow one from other localities, which, although inhabited by a race observing similar customs, may have been sunk in a state of barbarism at a time when it was civilised, or *vice versâ*. Each locality must yield its separate quota of evidence to its own careful observers, and until this has been effected in more districts than is at present the case, any attempt at generalization would only prove as fallacious as it would be unscientific.

To the rude stone monuments of Ireland those of Cornwall bear the most striking resemblance. There is, however, this difference between the two: that while the former country possesses in many instances a traditional history attaching to the barrows and cromlechs, the latter (with the exception of the solitary case of Rosemoddress) has lost it altogether.

This fact may be attributed in great measure to the preservation of the native Irish language on the one hand, and the decline and fall of the Cornish on the other.[1]

In conclusion, the author cannot do better than quote the words of Mr. Freeman,[2] who observes that, although "the sepulchral barrow can neither err nor lie, *we* must be constantly on our guard against our own misinterpretations." If, in the above remarks, he has misinterpreted the evidence at his disposal, he has at least supplied the reader with the facts in detail which led him to do so. These facts, since they are authentic, will retain their value to science, no matter how false the theories they have given rise to may hereafter be proved to be.[3]

---

[1] The epitaph of one of its latest spokesmen might well and truly be set up over the grave of each and every ancient Cornu-Briton, who in his death has carried with him not only the tale of the past, but the very language in which that tale was told:—

"Beneath this fair stone, the remains lie of one,
In the Cornish tongue skilled above all:
The day shall arrive, when his bones shall revive,
But the language is gone past recall."

In Cornish—"Dadn an Mean, ma Deskes broaz Dean,
En Tavaz Kernuak gelles,
Termen vedn doaz, rag an Corfe thethoras,
Mez Tavaz coth Kernow ew kellys."

The epitaph is to the memory of Mr. John Keigwin, written by Mr. Boson, of Newlyn, the 20th of April, 1716; and translated as above by Dr. Borlase. Mr. Keigwin died several years previously. (See *MS. Mems. of Corn. Tongue.* W.B. 1743).

[2] *Historical Essays*, p. 27.

[3] *Descent of Man*, vol. ii, p. 385. See Mr. Darwin's remark on *False Facts* and *False Views*.

Addenda.

(A.) SEPULCHRAL MONUMENTS IN MENEAGE.

On the 5th of July, 1872, the author accompanied Mr. Blight, sen., of Penzance, to visit some of the antiquities in the district known as Meneage. Than that gentleman there is no one who has paid greater attention to the objects of interest in the unexplored tract of country which forms the Lizard peninsula; and it is entirely through his kindness that the author is enabled to introduce the following descriptions, without which any notice of Cornish sepulchral remains would be incomplete.

The Map of the Goonhilly Downs, or that undulating expanse of wastrell which forms the central feature of this district, is dotted over in all directions with tumuli. Like those in the neighbourhood of St. Columb, they are of large size, and are sometimes placed in lines of three or four, sometimes singly on the summit of rising ground.

Almost all of them, as the author has been kindly informed by Sir Richard Vyvyan, Bart., of Trelowarren, were searched above a century ago. A few, however, still remain unexplored. In one of these, lately opened by the owner of the property, a large quantity of burnt earth was discovered, but no sepulchral remains.

The highest part of Goonhilly is known as the Dry Tree,[1] and is surmounted by three tumuli, on one of which a pole is fixed. Fifty yards to the north of this conspicuous object, and about the same distance from another barrow, is a stone 14 feet 7 inches in length, and 9 feet 8 inches in girth at the larger extremity, lying prostrate at the end of a shallow pit in which it evidently once stood upright. It is an unhewn bastard serpentine, somewhat dissimilar in its nature to other rocks in its immediate vicinity. When erect, it must have been an exceedingly fine Menhir, and was, doubtless, connected in some manner with the barrows which lie around it.

At a distance of three miles, as the crow flies,

---

[1] This name, like that of Dry Carn, in St. Just, probably alludes to the *three* tumuli, and not to the Surveyor's pole.

from the Dry Tree Stone, in the direction of St. Keverne, is the farm of Tremenheere. This place derives its name, (like the Tremenheere, in Ludgvan, previously mentioned,) from a fine unhewn monolith, the only one which still stands erect in the district,

MONOLITH AT TREMENHEERE, ST. KEVERNE.
From a Sketch by the Author.

situated in the pathway field leading from that village to St. Keverne.[1]

So finely proportioned, and symmetrical in its outline is this stone, that, although a tool has never

---

[1] There is a third farm called Tremenheere, in the parish of Sithians.

been used upon it, it might with justice be termed a handsome monument.

It is a diallage rock, measuring 9 feet 5 inches in height. In bulk, (at a distance of 2 feet 6 inches from the ground,) it measures 10 feet 10 inches, but tapers off towards the top. In its ground-plan it is triangular, having three faces, of which the southernmost is the widest. Judging from similar monuments in the West, it seems probable that it was on this latter and broader side that the interment took place. The ground, however, seems never to have been searched.

But the most interesting object in the parish of St. Keverne still remains to be described. It con-

THE THREE BROTHERS OF GRUGITH.
From a Sketch by the Author.

sists of a half natural, half artificial, dolmen or cromlech, situated on the estate of Grugith, on the Crowza Downs,—a wild marshy tract, strewn with diallage[1]

---

[1] See Sir H. De la Beche, *Geology of Cornwall, &c.*, p. 396.

rocks, each of them many tons in weight. In the locality it is known as the "Three Brothers of Grugith."

In the case of this monument, a natural rock *in situ*, 8 feet 8 inches long by six feet broad, and 2 feet 6 inches high, has been selected as the side-stone of the cromlech. At a distance of 2 feet 3 inches from it, and parallel to its northern side, a second stone 7 feet 4 inches long, and averaging from six to eighteen inches broad, has been set up on edge. A third stone, measuring 8 feet 3 inches by 5 feet 3 inches, has then been laid across the two. A Kist-Vaen, open at the ends, has thus been formed, 2 feet 3 inches deep, *i.e.* from the under side of the covering stone to the natural surface of the ground around it. Having obtained permission from Lord Falmouth to search the sepulchral monuments on his property in this district, the author caused a pit to be sunk between the supporters of the 'Quoit.' Nothing, however, was discovered besides a small flint chip,[1] and the fact that a similar pit had been sunk in the same spot to a depth of four feet from the surface, *previous to the erection of the structure.* This was, doubtless, a grave like that at Lanyon, which, if it

---

[1] The Author hopes at no distant opportunity to be able to give an account of the discovery of a remarkable deposit of chipped flints in this district, as well as some other traces of its very early occupation by man. At present, however, it is foreign to the subject of his work.

had not been subsequently disturbed, had, at all events, lost all trace of its ancient occupant.[1]

(B.) BOSKEDNAN CIRCLE.

It has been remarked at a previous page that, although there is no more proof that our megalithic circles were *in their origin* merely sepulchral monuments, than there is in the case of a church from the fact that interments were placed in and around it, still it is well worthy of notice that numerous barrows

BOSKEDNAN CIRCLE AND BARROW.
From a Sketch by the Author.

or cairns almost invariably occur in very close proximity to monuments of this class. A very good instance of a cairn situated on the very edge of a

---

[1] When he wrote his remarks on Cornish Cromlechs, (see page 15,) the Author had not visited this monument. Had he done so, he would have certainly mentioned it as an example of Cromlechs of the third class, such as that at Craig-Madden, in Stirlingshire.

circle, is to be found on the higher part of Boskednan on the Gulval Downs; and as the results of its exploration on the 26th of July, 1872, were curious, the author is induced to insert an account of it here.

This circle consisted in Borlase's time of nineteen stones, thirteen of which were then erect, with a detached "long-stone" forty-three paces to the north-west.[1] Eleven of these stones are all that now remain, seven of which are standing, while four are prostrate. Of those now standing the average height is four feet, with the exception of a fine menhir,[2] on the northern side, which measures 6 feet 6 inches above the surface of the ground. Immediately opposite this, at a distance of seventy feet, on the southern side of the ring, stands a flat-faced stone, about four feet high, the base of which is surrounded by the outskirts of a cairn, which thus is made to cut the circumference of the circle at this point. So large a portion of the stones composing it have been removed that neither its height nor circumference can now be determined. Thinking, however, that some object of interest might still be obtained among the *débris*, the author caused a trench to be dug across it; and the four side-stones of a Kist-Vaen were soon discovered.

---

[1] This is still to be found, though the top is broken off.

[2] The ground around this was carefully searched, but no interment discovered. The occurrence of single stones taller than the rest, in many of these circles, has been previously noticed.

This chamber stood in such a position that a line drawn due N. and S. from it to the Menhir on the northern side of the ring would immediately bisect the circle, and cut the flat-faced stone on the southern side, from the latter of which it was distant twenty-two feet. The measurements of the chamber were respectively: length, (from W.N.W. to E.S.E.,) four feet; breadth, 2 feet 6 inches; and depth (to the surface of a pavement neatly formed of three flat stones,) 1 foot 6 inches. The cover had been unfortunately removed, and the chamber rifled. Continuing the trench in a westerly direction, the workman discovered, at a distance of two feet from the Kist-Vaen, a large quantity of burnt wood; and two feet further still, the fragments of an urn, formed of very coarse clay. In shape and size the vessel was probably much like that found at Tredinney. The chevron pattern round the upper part was not unlike that on the first Angrowse Urn; but the bosses or handles, though neatly formed, were in slight relief and not perforated. The interior as well as the exterior of the rim showed the "twisted-cord" pattern so common to the sepulchral pottery in general, and the vessel seems to have differed little from the usual type. No bones or ashes were found with the fragments; and as one piece occurred near the present summit of the cairn, it may reasonably be supposed that the vessel, originally interred in the kist, had been broken by the workmen who discovered it, and the pieces carelessly thrown aside at the spot where they were rediscovered.

The remains of two other cairns are to be found at a distance of some 200 yards to the north-west of Boskednan Circle. "On the top" of one of these stood, in all probability, a Kist-Vaen mentioned in Borlase's MSS. (*Paroch. Mem.*, p. 9). He describes it as measuring "three-and-a-half feet wide, by six feet long, neatly walled on the two sides and the western end, (the eastern being broken up); across the top of it lies a flatt stone, three-and-a-half feet wide, and eight feet long. There was also formerly another covering stone, which, both together, secured the cavity, and what it contained."

Another large, but dilapidated cairn, is to be found at distance of 200 yards east of the same circle.[1]

(c.) BARROWS NEAR BOSPORTHENNIS, ZENNOR.

On the 14th of August, 1872, the author caused some barrows to be opened on the Downs to the east of the Hut-Circles at Bosporthennis. Two of

---

[1] For a drawing of the Boskednan Circle as it was one hundred years ago, see *Borlase's Antiquities*, Plate xiii, fig. ii.

these occupied the summit of a rising ground, at a distance of one hundred paces apart, in a line N. and S.; while a third was placed on the slope of the hill some 800 paces to the W.N.W.

All three of these tumuli had been previously dismantled by stone-carriers, the third being only *eighteen inches* in height. Enough, however, remained in each case to make a search worth while, and, accordingly, workmen were set to cut trenches through those on the top of the hill. Each of these proved to be "a ring barrow," (twenty-four feet in diameter) of the ordinary type. Circles of stones on edge had been placed round piles of natural rock, and over the surfaces of these the ashes of the funeral pile were still strewn in abundance. In the southernmost of the two was found a flint chip and a piece of iron, to the surface of which latter were adhering ashes and burnt earth. It seemed to have been preserved owing to its having passed through the fire.

Section of Concentric Circle Cairn, near Bosporthennis.
Scale, ⅛-of-an-inch to a foot.

No interments were discovered in either of the ring barrows; and it is therefore possible that they were simply burning-places for the bodies, which were subsequently interred at the third and last barrow now to be described.

The diameter of this cairn was thirty feet, and its height (as previously mentioned) eighteen inches. It was surrounded by a circle of stones on edge. On cutting a trench to the centre, a second and inner circle was discovered, measuring eight feet in diameter, and formed of stones set on end in the manner indicated in the section on the preceding page.

The western side of this inner ring was occupied by a single flat stone resting on the hard soil, and on

Two Urns found near Bosporthennis.
Restored by the Author from the fragments.

Fig. 1.
Diam. at mouth...... 10¾ inches.
Height (probably)... 10 inches.

Fig. 2.
Diam. at mouth...... 7¾ inches.
Height (probably)... 8 inches.

the eastern side stood (mouths downwards) the two urns here figured. Small stones had been carefully jammed in round them, but apparently no trouble had been taken to shield them from the débris of the superincumbent cairn.[1] They were therefore hopelessly crushed, or, as the Americans would say, "telescoped."

The sketches on the preceding page are therefore only restorations from the fragments. Both vessels were filled with burnt bones, among which roots had forced their way. Portions of the skull were clearly recognisable among these; and in the mouth of the larger urn was the little flint implement, of which a drawing is here given.

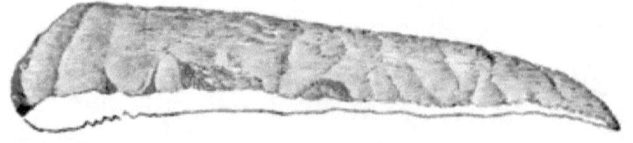

FLINT IMPLEMENT FOUND WITH THE LARGER URN, IN A CAIRN NEAR BOSPORTHENNIS.—ACTUAL SIZE.
From a Drawing by the Author.

Taken by itself this implement would come under the class known to the Pre-historic Archæologist as "awls;" but from the company in which it was found, the author believes it to have been simply the strike-a-light for the funeral pile. The marks of *secondary* chipping are very distinct, and it has passed through the fire.

The pottery of the urns is remarkable, from the

---

[1] It is possible, however, that the "cap stones" may have been removed by stone carriers.

fact that it bears a greater similarity, both in shape and make, to the black domestic ware found in the "hut-dwellings" than any hitherto noticed.[1] In both cases it is exceedingly thick and coarse at the lower extremity of the vessels, but is thinner and better made as it approaches the top.

The Zennor Circle, (figured by Borlase, *Ant.*, pl. xiii, and previously noticed as in all probability a sepulchral monument,) lies to the east of this same Downs.

---

[1] Some specimens of domestic pottery found with iron implements and Samian ware at Chapel Euny, as previously mentioned, are not distinguishable from the pottery of these urns.

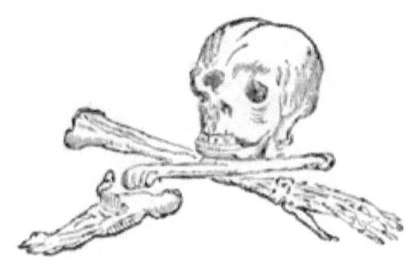

ERRATA.

Page 11, line 9, for "Ordinance," read "Ordnance." Page 31, note, for "page ," read "page 69." Page 33, last line, for "Cromlech!" read "cromlech." Page 40, note, for "page ," read "page 155." Page 49, note, for "Furgusson," read "Fergusson." Page 50, note, *id.* Page 54, line 24, for "however, that the," read "however, the." Page 78, line 9, for "p. note," read "p. 69 note." Page 116, line 14, for "most," read "almost." Page 177, line 4, for "Vaen," read "Vean." Page 178, line 3, *id.*

www.ingramcontent.com/pod-product-compliance
Lightning Source LLC
Chambersburg PA
CBHW031249250426
43672CB00029BA/1394